I0019733

Public Key Infrastructure: all you need to know about PKI

James Relington

Copyright © 2025 James Relington

All rights reserved

DEDICATION

This book is dedicated to all the professionals working tirelessly to secure digital identities and protect organizations from ever-evolving threats. To the cybersecurity teams, IT administrators, and identity management experts who ensure safe and seamless access for users— your work is invaluable. And to my family and friends, whose support and encouragement made this journey possible, thank you.

AKNOWLEDGEMENTS

I would like to express my deepest gratitude to everyone who contributed to the creation of this book. To my colleagues and mentors in the cybersecurity and identity management field, your insights and expertise have been invaluable. To the organizations and professionals who shared their experiences and best practices, your contributions have enriched this work. A special thanks to my family and friends for their unwavering support and encouragement throughout this journey. Finally, to the readers, thank you for your interest in identity lifecycle management—may this book help you navigate the evolving landscape of digital security with confidence.

Introduction to Public Key Infrastructure

Public Key Infrastructure (PKI) is the foundation of secure communications and digital trust in modern computing. It enables encryption, authentication, and integrity through the use of cryptographic keys and digital certificates. As cyber threats continue to evolve, PKI remains a critical component in securing networks, transactions, and sensitive data. Understanding PKI is essential for organizations and individuals who rely on digital security mechanisms to protect their assets and communications.

PKI operates on the principle of asymmetric cryptography, which involves a pair of cryptographic keys: a public key and a private key. These keys work together to encrypt and decrypt information, ensuring that only authorized parties can access or verify data. The public key is openly shared, allowing anyone to encrypt a message, but only the owner of the corresponding private key can decrypt it. This approach enhances security by eliminating the need to share secret encryption keys, as required in symmetric cryptography.

A core element of PKI is the digital certificate, which binds a public key to an entity's identity, such as an individual, organization, or website. These certificates are issued by trusted third parties known as Certificate Authorities (CAs). A CA verifies the identity of the certificate requester before issuing a certificate, ensuring that the public key truly belongs to the entity it claims to represent. Digital certificates provide authenticity and integrity, preventing unauthorized entities from impersonating legitimate users or services.

The process of obtaining and managing digital certificates follows a structured lifecycle. This begins with a certificate request, where an entity generates a key pair and submits a request to a CA. The CA verifies the request, issues the certificate, and publishes it for use. Once issued, a certificate must be carefully managed to ensure its validity. Expired or compromised certificates can pose significant security risks, which is why organizations must implement certificate lifecycle management strategies, including renewal and revocation mechanisms.

To maintain trust in a PKI system, certificate revocation plays a crucial role. If a private key is compromised, or if an entity no longer requires a certificate, it must be revoked to prevent misuse. CAs maintain a Certificate Revocation List (CRL) or provide Online Certificate Status Protocol (OCSP) services to inform users about invalid certificates. These mechanisms help prevent security breaches by ensuring that revoked certificates are not mistakenly trusted.

PKI extends beyond basic encryption and authentication. It plays a critical role in securing web communications through SSL/TLS certificates, which are used to establish secure HTTPS connections between web browsers and servers. These certificates ensure that data transmitted over the internet remains private and unaltered. Without PKI, online transactions, banking, and secure email communications would be vulnerable to interception and fraud.

Organizations implement PKI to secure access control, ensuring that only authorized users can access specific systems or resources. Through smart cards, USB tokens, and biometric authentication, PKI strengthens identity verification processes. It is widely used in enterprise environments for Single Sign-On (SSO) solutions, allowing employees to authenticate securely without managing multiple passwords.

Digital signatures are another significant application of PKI. They allow users to sign electronic documents with cryptographic proof of authenticity and integrity. A digital signature verifies that a document has not been altered since it was signed and that the signer is legitimate. This is crucial for legal, financial, and governmental transactions where trust and non-repudiation are required.

The security of PKI itself depends on several factors, including the protection of private keys, the trustworthiness of CAs, and the integrity of the entire PKI ecosystem. If a CA is compromised, the trust in certificates it has issued is broken, potentially leading to security breaches. To mitigate risks, organizations implement strict security policies, use Hardware Security Modules (HSMs) to store private keys, and adopt multi-layered authentication mechanisms.

Despite its robustness, PKI is not without challenges. Managing a large number of certificates can be complex, requiring automated solutions to track expirations, renewals, and revocations. Additionally, the rise of quantum computing poses a potential threat to PKI, as quantum computers could break current cryptographic algorithms. Researchers are actively working on quantum-resistant cryptographic solutions to ensure that PKI remains viable in the future.

As digital transformation accelerates, PKI continues to evolve, integrating with emerging technologies such as blockchain, Internet of Things (IoT), and cloud computing. These integrations enhance security frameworks while ensuring scalability and adaptability in modern IT infrastructures. Organizations across industries, from finance to healthcare, rely on PKI to secure transactions, protect sensitive data, and maintain regulatory compliance.

Understanding PKI is fundamental for anyone working with cybersecurity, IT infrastructure, or digital trust mechanisms. Whether securing web communications, authenticating users, or signing digital documents, PKI serves as the backbone of modern security. Its ability to establish trust in an untrusted environment makes it an indispensable technology for protecting sensitive information in an increasingly interconnected world.

History and Evolution of PKI

Public Key Infrastructure (PKI) has become a fundamental pillar of modern digital security, providing authentication, encryption, and trust mechanisms in various applications. However, its development was not sudden but rather a result of decades of cryptographic research and technological advancements. The history of PKI is deeply intertwined with the evolution of cryptography, the rise of the internet, and the growing need for secure communications in both government and commercial sectors.

The roots of PKI trace back to the development of asymmetric cryptography in the 1970s. Before this period, cryptography relied entirely on symmetric key algorithms, where both the sender and receiver used the same key for encryption and decryption. While effective, symmetric encryption posed significant challenges in securely exchanging keys, especially over untrusted networks. The need for a more scalable and secure method of encryption led to the birth of public-key cryptography.

In 1976, Whitfield Diffie and Martin Hellman introduced the concept of public-key cryptography in their groundbreaking paper New Directions in Cryptography. Their work proposed the use of two mathematically linked keys: a public key for encryption and a private key for decryption. This innovation eliminated the need for secure key exchange, allowing anyone to encrypt messages while ensuring that only the intended recipient could decrypt them. Although their method was revolutionary, it did not provide an efficient digital signature mechanism or practical implementation.

Shortly after, in 1977, Ronald Rivest, Adi Shamir, and Leonard Adleman developed the RSA algorithm, which became the first widely adopted public-key cryptographic system. RSA enabled both encryption and digital signatures, laying the foundation for secure online communication. Its introduction marked the beginning of a new era in cryptography and played a crucial role in the eventual development of PKI.

The next major milestone in PKI's evolution occurred in the 1980s with the creation of digital certificates. As public-key cryptography gained traction, there was a growing need for a system that could verify the authenticity of public keys. The concept of a trusted third party, known as a Certificate Authority (CA), emerged to address this issue. A CA would issue digital certificates to bind an entity's identity to its public key, ensuring trust in online interactions. This idea was formalized in the X.509 certificate standard, which remains a core component of PKI today.

By the 1990s, the rapid expansion of the internet highlighted the necessity of a structured PKI system. With businesses and governments increasingly relying on digital communications, securing sensitive data became a top priority. The rise of e-commerce, online banking, and secure email communications fueled the adoption of PKI-based solutions. Secure Sockets Layer (SSL) certificates, introduced by Netscape in 1995, became a critical application of PKI, enabling secure encrypted connections between web servers and browsers.

Governments also recognized the importance of PKI in national security and electronic governance. Various countries began developing PKI frameworks to support secure identity verification, digital signatures, and encrypted communications for citizens and businesses. The U.S. government, for instance, launched the Federal PKI initiative to standardize digital certificates for government agencies and contractors.

The early 2000s saw an increasing reliance on PKI across multiple industries. Organizations implemented PKI for enterprise security, using digital certificates to authenticate employees, secure internal networks, and protect confidential information. The financial sector leveraged PKI to enable secure transactions and online banking, ensuring compliance with regulatory requirements.

Despite its growing adoption, PKI also faced challenges, including certificate management complexities and security concerns. The need to track certificate lifecycles, prevent expired or compromised certificates from being used, and ensure the integrity of certificate authorities led to the development of automated certificate management solutions. Organizations began adopting best practices for certificate issuance, revocation, and renewal to mitigate risks associated with expired or fraudulent certificates.

Another critical moment in the history of PKI came with the introduction of new cryptographic threats. Advances in computing power made some older cryptographic algorithms vulnerable to attacks. Weak encryption standards, such as the early versions of SSL, were gradually replaced with stronger protocols like Transport Layer Security (TLS). Additionally, the rise of quantum computing posed a potential future threat to traditional public-key algorithms, prompting researchers to explore post-quantum cryptography to secure PKI systems against emerging threats.

As technology continued to evolve, PKI expanded beyond traditional applications. The rise of cloud computing, mobile devices, and the Internet of Things (IoT) required PKI to adapt to new environments. Cloud-based PKI services emerged, offering scalable and flexible solutions for managing digital certificates. IoT devices, which often lacked robust security mechanisms, began incorporating PKI for authentication and secure communication, preventing unauthorized access and data breaches.

The integration of PKI with blockchain technology also became a topic of interest. While blockchain offers decentralized trust mechanisms, PKI provides authentication and encryption features that complement distributed ledger technologies. Some blockchain implementations utilize PKI for secure identity management and transaction verification, enhancing trust in digital ecosystems.

Today, PKI remains an essential component of cybersecurity, supporting authentication, encryption, and integrity in various digital interactions. It is widely used in secure web browsing, electronic signatures, cloud security, and identity management. As cyber threats become more sophisticated, PKI continues to evolve, incorporating new technologies and security standards to maintain trust in an increasingly digital world.

The journey of PKI, from its theoretical foundations in the 1970s to its widespread adoption in the modern era, highlights its critical role in securing digital communications. Its evolution reflects the ongoing need for trust and security in an interconnected world, ensuring that sensitive data and transactions remain protected against ever-evolving cyber threats.

Fundamentals of Cryptography

Cryptography is the science of securing communication and information through mathematical techniques that ensure confidentiality, integrity, authentication, and non-repudiation. It has been used for centuries to protect sensitive information, evolving from simple ciphers used in ancient civilizations to complex algorithms that secure modern digital communications. As technology advances, cryptography remains an essential tool for securing data in transit and at rest, forming the foundation of Public Key Infrastructure (PKI) and various cybersecurity mechanisms.

At its core, cryptography relies on the concept of encryption, which transforms readable data, known as plaintext, into an unreadable format called ciphertext. Only authorized parties with the correct decryption key can revert the ciphertext back to its original form. The process of encryption and decryption ensures that sensitive information remains protected from unauthorized access, even if it is intercepted by malicious actors. Encryption plays a vital role in securing online transactions, email communications, cloud storage, and digital identity management.

There are two primary types of encryption: symmetric and asymmetric. Symmetric encryption uses a single key for both encryption and decryption. This means that both the sender and receiver must have access to the same key, requiring a secure method of key exchange. Symmetric algorithms, such as the Advanced Encryption Standard (AES) and Triple Data Encryption Standard (3DES), are widely used for securing data at rest and in high-speed network encryption. While symmetric encryption is efficient, its major drawback is the difficulty of securely sharing and managing encryption keys in large-scale environments.

Asymmetric encryption, also known as public-key cryptography, solves the key exchange problem by using two mathematically related keys: a public key and a private key. The public key is shared openly, allowing anyone to encrypt data, but only the corresponding private key can decrypt it. This approach enhances security by eliminating the need to exchange secret keys over insecure channels. The Rivest-Shamir-Adleman (RSA) algorithm and Elliptic Curve Cryptography (ECC) are common examples of asymmetric encryption, widely used in PKI, digital signatures, and secure online communications.

One of the key principles of cryptography is data integrity, which ensures that information has not been altered or tampered with during transmission or storage. Hash functions play a crucial role in verifying data integrity by generating a fixed-length cryptographic hash from input data. Even a minor change in the original data results in a significantly different hash value, making it easy to detect modifications. Secure hash algorithms, such as SHA-256 and SHA-3, are commonly used in digital signatures, password storage, and blockchain technology to maintain data integrity.

Authentication is another fundamental aspect of cryptography, ensuring that entities involved in communication or transactions are legitimate. Digital signatures provide a way to verify the authenticity and integrity of digital messages, documents, and software. A digital signature is generated using the sender's private key and can be verified by anyone using the corresponding public key. If the signature is valid, it confirms that the message originated from the stated sender and has not been altered. Digital signatures are widely used in email security, software distribution, and legal document verification.

Non-repudiation is an essential security property that prevents entities from denying their actions or commitments. In the context of cryptography, non-repudiation ensures that a sender cannot deny having signed a digital document or sent a specific message. This is particularly important in financial transactions, legal contracts, and electronic voting systems, where proof of origin and authenticity must be maintained. By using cryptographic techniques like digital signatures and timestamping, organizations can ensure accountability and trust in digital interactions.

Key management is a critical component of cryptographic security, as the strength of encryption depends on the confidentiality and proper handling of cryptographic keys. Secure key generation, storage, distribution, and revocation are necessary to prevent unauthorized access and key compromise. Hardware Security Modules (HSMs) and Key Management Systems (KMS) provide secure environments for generating and storing cryptographic keys, reducing the risk of exposure to cyber threats. Poor key management practices can undermine even the strongest encryption algorithms, making it essential to implement best practices for key lifecycle management.

Cryptographic protocols combine various cryptographic techniques to provide secure communication and authentication in digital environments. Protocols such as Transport Layer Security (TLS), Secure Shell (SSH), and Internet Protocol Security (IPsec) leverage encryption, authentication, and integrity mechanisms to protect data transmission over networks. TLS, for example, is the foundation of HTTPS, ensuring that web browsers and servers establish encrypted connections for secure online transactions. Cryptographic protocols play a crucial role in securing remote access, virtual private networks (VPNs), and wireless communications.

As cryptographic technology continues to evolve, so do the threats and challenges associated with it. Advances in computing power, particularly with the development of quantum computers, pose potential risks to traditional encryption algorithms. Quantum computers have the capability to break widely used asymmetric cryptographic schemes, such as RSA and ECC, by efficiently solving complex mathematical problems that would take classical computers an impractical amount of time. Researchers are actively working on post-quantum cryptography, developing new algorithms resistant to quantum attacks to ensure the future security of cryptographic systems.

The role of cryptography extends beyond cybersecurity and into emerging technologies such as blockchain, artificial intelligence, and the Internet of Things (IoT). Blockchain relies on cryptographic hash functions and digital signatures to secure transactions and maintain decentralized trust. IoT devices use cryptographic methods to authenticate and encrypt communications, preventing unauthorized access and data breaches. As organizations continue to adopt digital transformation strategies, cryptography remains a fundamental pillar of secure and trustworthy systems.

The fundamentals of cryptography are essential to understanding how modern security mechanisms protect digital assets and communications. By leveraging encryption, authentication, and integrity verification, cryptography ensures that sensitive data remains secure in an increasingly interconnected world. As cyber threats evolve, continuous advancements in cryptographic research and implementation are necessary to maintain trust and security in digital ecosystems.

Symmetric vs Asymmetric Encryption

Encryption is a fundamental aspect of cryptography, ensuring the confidentiality of information by transforming readable data into an unreadable format that can only be deciphered by authorized parties. The two primary types of encryption used in modern security systems are symmetric and asymmetric encryption. Each method has its own strengths, weaknesses, and use cases, making it essential to understand their differences and how they contribute to secure communication and data protection.

Symmetric encryption is the oldest and simplest form of encryption, relying on a single key for both encryption and decryption. The sender and the recipient must share the same secret key, which is used to encode and decode the message. This type of encryption is highly efficient, making it ideal for encrypting large volumes of data quickly. Some of the most widely used symmetric encryption algorithms include the Advanced Encryption Standard (AES), Triple Data Encryption Standard (3DES), and the legacy Data Encryption Standard (DES). These algorithms are commonly employed in securing file storage, database encryption, and high-speed network communications.

One of the key advantages of symmetric encryption is its speed and efficiency. Because the same key is used for both encryption and decryption, the computational overhead is minimal, allowing for faster processing compared to asymmetric encryption. This efficiency makes symmetric encryption suitable for securing real-time applications, such as voice and video calls, as well as encrypting large files and databases where performance is a critical factor.

Despite its advantages, symmetric encryption has a significant drawback: key distribution. Since both parties need access to the same encryption key, securely exchanging and managing the key becomes a challenge, especially in large-scale environments. If the key is intercepted or compromised during transmission, an attacker can decrypt all encrypted messages, rendering the security ineffective. This limitation makes symmetric encryption less practical for secure communication over untrusted networks, such as the internet, where key exchange can be a major security risk.

To address the challenges of key exchange, asymmetric encryption was developed. Unlike symmetric encryption, asymmetric encryption uses a pair of mathematically related keys: a public key and a private key. The public key is openly shared and used for encryption, while the private key is kept secret and used for decryption. This approach eliminates the need for both parties to share a single secret key, reducing the risks associated with key distribution.

The most well-known asymmetric encryption algorithm is the Rivest-Shamir-Adleman (RSA) algorithm, which has been widely used for secure communications, digital signatures, and authentication systems. Other commonly used asymmetric encryption methods include Elliptic Curve Cryptography (ECC) and the Diffie-Hellman key exchange protocol. These cryptographic techniques enable secure data exchange, even over untrusted networks, by ensuring that only the intended recipient can decrypt the information.

Asymmetric encryption provides a higher level of security compared to symmetric encryption, particularly in scenarios where secure key exchange is required. Because the private key remains confidential, an attacker who intercepts the public key cannot decrypt the message without access to the private key. This makes asymmetric encryption ideal for securing web communications, email encryption, and digital signatures, where authentication and confidentiality are critical.

However, the primary disadvantage of asymmetric encryption is its computational complexity. The encryption and decryption processes in asymmetric cryptography require significantly more processing power than symmetric encryption, making it slower and less efficient for encrypting large amounts of data. This performance drawback limits the use of asymmetric encryption in scenarios requiring high-speed encryption, such as encrypting entire databases or streaming data in real-time.

To overcome the limitations of both encryption methods, modern security protocols often use a combination of symmetric and asymmetric encryption. This hybrid approach leverages the strengths of each method to achieve both security and efficiency. In a typical implementation, asymmetric encryption is used to securely exchange a symmetric key between parties, and then symmetric encryption is used to encrypt the actual data. This is the approach taken by protocols such as Secure Sockets Layer (SSL) and Transport Layer Security (TLS), which secure web communications by using asymmetric encryption for key exchange and symmetric encryption for data transmission.

Another application where the combination of symmetric and asymmetric encryption is widely used is in secure email communication. Pretty Good Privacy (PGP) and Secure/Multipurpose

Internet Mail Extensions (S/MIME) use asymmetric encryption to protect email content and symmetric encryption to efficiently encrypt large email attachments. This ensures that email messages remain confidential while maintaining efficient encryption processing.

In addition to secure communication, asymmetric encryption plays a vital role in authentication and digital signatures. Digital signatures use asymmetric cryptography to verify the authenticity of messages or documents, ensuring that the sender is legitimate and that the content has not been altered. This is critical in online banking, software distribution, and legal document signing, where trust and non-repudiation are essential.

The ongoing advancements in computing power and cryptographic research continue to influence the development of new encryption techniques. While symmetric encryption remains the preferred choice for encrypting large volumes of data due to its speed, asymmetric encryption is crucial for securing key exchanges, authentication, and digital identities. The rise of quantum computing also presents new challenges for traditional encryption methods, prompting the development of quantum-resistant cryptographic algorithms to ensure long-term security.

Both symmetric and asymmetric encryption play an indispensable role in modern cybersecurity, each addressing different security needs. Understanding when to use each encryption method and how to combine them effectively is essential for building secure systems that protect sensitive information against evolving cyber threats.

Understanding Public and Private Keys

Public and private keys form the foundation of modern cryptographic security, enabling secure communication, authentication, and data protection in digital environments. These keys are essential components of asymmetric encryption, a cryptographic method that eliminates the need for a shared secret key by using a pair of mathematically linked keys. Understanding how public and private keys function, their relationship, and their various applications is critical for anyone working with cybersecurity, cryptography, or digital identity management.

At the core of asymmetric encryption is the concept of key pairs. Unlike symmetric encryption, where the same key is used for both encryption and decryption, asymmetric encryption employs two separate but mathematically related keys. One of these is the public key, which can be freely shared and used to encrypt messages. The other is the private key, which is kept secret and is required for decryption. This key pair ensures that encrypted data remains secure, as only the owner of the private key can decrypt messages encrypted with the corresponding public key.

The relationship between public and private keys is based on complex mathematical functions that are easy to compute in one direction but extremely difficult to reverse without the correct key. This principle, known as a "one-way function," ensures that even if an attacker obtains the public key, they cannot derive the private key from it. Common cryptographic algorithms that use public and private keys include RSA (Rivest-Shamir-Adleman), Elliptic Curve Cryptography (ECC), and Diffie-Hellman key exchange. These algorithms rely on mathematical problems, such as prime factorization and discrete logarithms, which are computationally infeasible to solve within a reasonable timeframe using classical computing methods.

One of the primary uses of public and private keys is secure communication. When two parties need to exchange sensitive information over an untrusted network, they can use asymmetric encryption to ensure confidentiality. For example, if a sender wants to send an encrypted message to a recipient, they use the recipient's public key to encrypt the message. Once encrypted, the message can only be decrypted by the recipient using their private key. This ensures that even if an attacker intercepts the message during transmission, they will not be able to read its contents.

Another critical application of public and private keys is authentication. Digital signatures, which are used to verify the authenticity and integrity of messages or documents, rely on asymmetric cryptography. When an individual or organization signs a digital document, they use their private key to generate a unique digital signature. Anyone can then use the corresponding public key to verify that the signature is valid and that the document has not been altered.

This mechanism is widely used in software distribution, online transactions, and legal contracts to establish trust and prevent fraud.

Public and private keys also play a crucial role in securing web communications. The Transport Layer Security (TLS) protocol, which encrypts internet traffic to protect data from eavesdropping and tampering, uses asymmetric encryption to establish a secure connection between a client and a server. When a user visits a website with HTTPS, the web browser retrieves the website's public key from its digital certificate, issued by a trusted Certificate Authority (CA). The browser then encrypts a session key using the website's public key, and the server uses its private key to decrypt it. This exchange allows both parties to establish a secure communication channel, ensuring the confidentiality of transmitted data.

In addition to communication security, public and private keys are used for identity verification and access control. Organizations implement Public Key Infrastructure (PKI) to manage digital certificates that link public keys to individuals or devices. These certificates are used in smart cards, security tokens, and two-factor authentication (2FA) systems to enhance security. For example, employees may use a smart card containing a private key to log into a secure system, with the authentication server verifying their identity using the corresponding public key.

Despite their advantages, public and private keys must be managed carefully to maintain security. The private key must always remain confidential, as its compromise would allow attackers to decrypt sensitive data, forge digital signatures, or impersonate legitimate users. Organizations often use Hardware Security Modules (HSMs) to store private keys securely, reducing the risk of exposure. Additionally, key rotation policies ensure that cryptographic keys are periodically replaced to mitigate potential security vulnerabilities.

The security of public and private keys also depends on the strength of the cryptographic algorithms used. While RSA has been a dominant asymmetric encryption method for decades, it requires large key sizes to maintain security against modern computing power. ECC, on the other hand, provides the same level of security with smaller key sizes, making it more efficient and widely adopted in modern cryptographic implementations. As quantum computing continues to advance, researchers are developing post-quantum cryptographic algorithms to ensure that public-key cryptography remains secure against emerging threats.

Public and private keys are integral to digital security, enabling encryption, authentication, and secure access to systems. Their ability to facilitate secure communications without requiring direct key exchanges makes them essential for protecting sensitive data and maintaining trust in digital interactions. As cybersecurity threats evolve, the continued development and adoption of robust public-key cryptographic techniques will remain critical for safeguarding information in an increasingly connected world.

Digital Certificates Explained

Digital certificates are a fundamental component of modern cybersecurity, providing a mechanism for establishing trust and authenticity in online communications. They are used to verify identities, encrypt data, and ensure the integrity of transmitted information. Without digital certificates, secure communications over the internet would be nearly impossible, leaving users vulnerable to cyber threats such as man-in-the-middle attacks, identity spoofing, and unauthorized data access. Understanding digital certificates, their structure, functions, and use cases is essential for anyone involved in cybersecurity, cryptography, or secure online transactions.

A digital certificate is an electronic document that binds a public key to an entity's identity. This entity can be an individual, an organization, a website, or even a device. The certificate serves as a digital passport that proves the legitimacy of the entity to anyone who interacts with it. Digital certificates are issued by trusted third parties known as Certificate Authorities (CAs), which play a crucial role in verifying the authenticity of certificate requests before granting them. The certificate itself contains key information, including the public key, the entity's details, the CA's digital signature, and the certificate's expiration date.

One of the primary purposes of digital certificates is to enable secure encrypted communication. When a user visits a secure website that uses HTTPS, their web browser checks the site's digital certificate to ensure that it is valid and issued by a trusted CA. If the certificate is legitimate, the browser establishes an encrypted connection using Transport Layer Security (TLS), ensuring that all data exchanged between the user and the website remains private and protected from attackers. This process prevents malicious actors from intercepting sensitive information such as login credentials, credit card details, and personal data.

The structure of a digital certificate follows the X.509 standard, which defines the format and content of certificates used in Public Key Infrastructure (PKI). Each certificate contains essential fields, including the subject name (the entity's identity), the issuer name (the CA that issued the certificate), the certificate serial number, the validity period, the public key, and the CA's digital signature. The digital signature is a cryptographic proof that the certificate was issued by a trusted authority and has not been tampered with. If a certificate's digital signature is invalid or altered, it will be rejected by the system verifying it.

Certificates are categorized into different types based on their intended use and level of validation. The most common types include domain validation (DV) certificates, organization validation (OV) certificates, and extended validation (EV) certificates. DV certificates provide basic encryption for websites and only verify domain ownership. OV certificates require additional verification of the organization's identity and are used by businesses and enterprises to establish trust. EV certificates undergo the highest level of validation, ensuring that the organization is legitimate and providing visual indicators, such as a green address bar in some browsers, to signal enhanced trust.

Another critical function of digital certificates is digital signatures, which ensure the authenticity and integrity of electronic documents, emails, and software. When a document is signed using a digital certificate, the recipient can verify the signature using the sender's public key. This process confirms that the document was signed by the stated sender and has not been altered since signing. Digital signatures are widely used in legal documents, software distribution, and secure email communications to prevent forgery and tampering.

The lifecycle of a digital certificate includes several key stages: issuance, usage, renewal, and revocation. Once issued by a CA, a certificate remains valid for a specific period, typically ranging from one to three years. Before it expires, it must be renewed to ensure continuous security. If a certificate's private key is compromised, or if the entity it represents is no longer trustworthy, the certificate must be revoked. Revoked certificates are added to a Certificate Revocation List (CRL) or checked in real-time using the Online Certificate Status Protocol (OCSP) to prevent their continued use.

Despite their advantages, digital certificates also come with challenges. Managing certificates at scale can be complex, especially for organizations that rely on thousands of certificates for different systems and applications. Expired certificates can cause security disruptions, leading to website downtime or compromised security. Automated certificate management solutions help mitigate these risks by tracking expiration dates, renewing certificates automatically, and ensuring compliance with security policies.

Security threats targeting digital certificates have also emerged over time. Attackers have exploited weaknesses in outdated cryptographic algorithms, such as SHA-1, leading to the transition to stronger algorithms like SHA-256. Additionally, fraudulent certificates issued by compromised or untrusted CAs have been used in cyberattacks to impersonate legitimate websites. To counter these threats, the industry has implemented stricter certificate issuance policies, multi-factor authentication for CA administrators, and improved transparency measures such as Certificate Transparency (CT) logs.

The future of digital certificates is evolving with advancements in cryptography and cybersecurity. The rise of quantum computing poses potential risks to current encryption methods, prompting research into quantum-resistant cryptographic algorithms that can replace traditional PKI systems. Additionally, emerging technologies such as blockchain are being explored for decentralized and tamper-proof certificate issuance and verification. These innovations aim to enhance the reliability and security of digital certificates in an increasingly digital world.

Digital certificates are an essential component of modern security infrastructure, enabling encrypted communication, authentication, and digital trust. Their role in securing online transactions, protecting data integrity, and verifying identities makes them indispensable in an era where cybersecurity threats continue to evolve. As technology advances, maintaining the integrity and security of digital certificates remains a top priority for organizations, governments, and individuals seeking to protect sensitive information in a connected world.

Certificate Authorities (CAs) and Their Role

Certificate Authorities (CAs) play a critical role in establishing trust in digital communications by issuing, verifying, and managing digital certificates. These certificates are fundamental components of Public Key Infrastructure (PKI), enabling encryption, authentication, and secure exchanges of information over the internet. Without CAs, it would be difficult to determine whether a website, email sender, or software package is legitimate, increasing the risk of identity theft, fraud, and cyberattacks. The function of a CA is to act as a trusted third party that ensures entities using digital certificates are who they claim to be.

At the core of a CA's responsibility is the issuance of digital certificates. When an individual, organization, or website applies for a certificate, the CA verifies their identity before issuing a certificate that binds their public key to their digital identity. This verification process varies depending on the level of trust required. For basic encryption, such as in domain validation (DV) certificates, the CA only confirms that the applicant controls the domain. However, for higher assurance certificates, such as organization validation (OV) and extended validation (EV) certificates, the CA conducts thorough background checks to ensure the legitimacy of the requesting entity.

The issuance process begins with a certificate request, where an applicant generates a cryptographic key pair and submits a Certificate Signing Request (CSR) to the CA. The CSR contains the public key and other identifying information about the entity requesting the certificate. The CA then evaluates the request based on its validation policies. If the request meets all security and identity requirements, the CA digitally signs the certificate using its own private key, creating a chain of trust. The certificate is then issued and can be used for secure communications, digital signatures, and authentication purposes.

Trust in a CA is established through a hierarchical system known as the certificate chain or trust chain. At the top of this hierarchy are root CAs, which are self-signed and form the foundation of trust. These root certificates are embedded in operating systems, web browsers, and other software to ensure automatic trust in certificates issued by them. Beneath the root CAs are intermediate CAs, which are delegated the authority to issue certificates on behalf of the root CA. This structure enhances security by ensuring that root certificates remain protected and are not directly involved in routine certificate issuance.

The role of CAs extends beyond issuing certificates; they are also responsible for maintaining certificate validity and managing revocations. If a certificate becomes compromised or is no longer trustworthy, it must be revoked to prevent its continued use. CAs publish lists of revoked certificates in a Certificate Revocation List (CRL) or provide real-time verification through the Online Certificate Status Protocol (OCSP). These mechanisms allow users and systems to check whether a certificate is still valid before trusting it, reducing the risk of security breaches.

CAs also play a key role in securing web traffic through the issuance of Secure Sockets Layer (SSL) and Transport Layer Security (TLS) certificates. These certificates enable encrypted HTTPS connections between web browsers and servers, protecting users from eavesdropping and man-in-the-middle attacks. When a user visits a secure website, their browser verifies the certificate against the trusted CA's root certificate. If the certificate is valid and trusted, the browser establishes a secure connection, ensuring that any data transmitted remains confidential and untampered.

In addition to securing websites, CAs issue certificates for email encryption, code signing, and device authentication. Email certificates, such as those used in S/MIME (Secure/Multipurpose Internet Mail Extensions), allow users to sign and encrypt emails, ensuring that messages are not altered or intercepted. Code signing certificates verify the authenticity of software and applications, preventing attackers from distributing malicious code disguised as legitimate software.

Device authentication certificates secure Internet of Things (IoT) devices, ensuring that only authorized devices can communicate within a network.

Despite their importance, CAs themselves are high-value targets for cybercriminals. If a CA is compromised, attackers can issue fraudulent certificates that appear legitimate, potentially enabling phishing attacks, man-in-the-middle attacks, or malware distribution. High-profile incidents, such as the breaches of DigiNotar and Comodo, have demonstrated the risks associated with CA security failures. To mitigate these risks, CAs implement strict security measures, including hardware security modules (HSMs) to protect private keys, multi-factor authentication for CA administrators, and regular security audits to detect vulnerabilities.

Another challenge associated with CAs is the potential for misuse or overreach. Governments and intelligence agencies have been known to exploit CA systems to issue surveillance certificates, allowing them to intercept encrypted communications. This has led to increased scrutiny of CA operations and the implementation of transparency measures, such as Certificate Transparency (CT) logs. These publicly accessible logs record all issued certificates, allowing security researchers and organizations to detect unauthorized or fraudulent certificates.

To further strengthen trust in digital certificates, the industry follows strict guidelines and compliance standards, such as the CA/Browser Forum's Baseline Requirements. These requirements dictate best practices for certificate issuance, validation, and security controls. Organizations that operate CAs must undergo regular audits to maintain compliance with these industry standards, ensuring that they continue to be trusted by browsers, operating systems, and other software vendors.

The future of CAs and digital certificates is evolving with advancements in cryptographic technology and cybersecurity threats. As quantum computing becomes more feasible, traditional cryptographic algorithms used by CAs may become vulnerable to quantum attacks. Researchers are actively developing quantum-resistant algorithms to ensure that PKI and CA systems remain secure in the post-quantum era. Additionally, new models of trust, such as decentralized and blockchain-based identity systems, are being explored as alternatives to traditional CA-based trust models.

Certificate Authorities serve as the backbone of digital trust, enabling secure communications, authentication, and data protection across the internet and enterprise environments. Their role in issuing, managing, and revoking digital certificates ensures that users can verify identities, encrypt sensitive information, and protect against cyber threats. As technology and security risks continue to evolve, the need for reliable, secure, and transparent CAs remains a cornerstone of global cybersecurity efforts.

Registration Authorities (RAs) and Their Importance

Registration Authorities (RAs) play a vital role in Public Key Infrastructure (PKI) by acting as intermediaries between users and Certificate Authorities (CAs). Their primary responsibility is to verify the identity of certificate applicants before they are issued a digital certificate. While CAs are responsible for generating and signing certificates, RAs ensure that the applicants meet the necessary requirements before a certificate is granted. This separation of duties enhances security, prevents fraudulent certificate issuance, and ensures that digital identities remain trustworthy.

In PKI, digital certificates serve as a mechanism to bind a public key to an entity's identity. However, before issuing a certificate, a CA must confirm that the request is legitimate. Since CAs often serve a large number of users and organizations across different locations, verifying each request manually would be impractical. This is where RAs come in. They are responsible for handling identity verification, approving or rejecting certificate requests, and forwarding approved requests to the CA for final issuance. By distributing these responsibilities, RAs enhance the efficiency and security of certificate management.

The verification process conducted by an RA depends on the type of certificate being requested. For basic domain validation (DV) certificates, the RA only needs to confirm that the applicant controls the domain in question, often through email verification or DNS records. However, for higher assurance certificates, such as organization validation (OV) and extended validation (EV) certificates, the RA must conduct more rigorous identity checks. These checks may include verifying business registration details, confirming legal entity status, and even performing face-to-face identity verification for individuals.

RAs are especially critical in large organizations, government institutions, and enterprises that require a high volume of digital certificates for employees, systems, and devices. Instead of relying solely on external CAs, these organizations establish internal RAs to streamline the certificate issuance process. An internal RA can authenticate employees and devices within the organization and submit validated requests to the CA for certificate generation. This approach not only speeds up the issuance process but also ensures that sensitive certificate requests do not need to be processed by an external authority.

Another important function of RAs is their role in certificate renewal and revocation. Digital certificates have a limited validity period, after which they must be renewed to maintain security. Before renewal, an RA verifies whether the original certificate holder is still authorized to receive a new certificate. If an entity no longer meets the necessary requirements or has changed ownership, the RA may reject the renewal request. Similarly, if a certificate's private key is compromised, the RA plays a role in initiating the revocation process, ensuring that the compromised certificate is added to the Certificate Revocation List (CRL) or flagged through the Online Certificate Status Protocol (OCSP).

Security is a major concern in certificate management, and RAs play a crucial role in enforcing policies that prevent unauthorized access to digital identities. By acting as a gatekeeper for certificate requests, RAs help prevent fraudulent certificate issuance. If an attacker were to gain access to an organization's CA directly, they could issue fake certificates for phishing or man-in-the-middle attacks. However, by requiring all requests to pass through an RA, the likelihood of unauthorized certificate issuance is significantly reduced.

In multi-tiered PKI architectures, RAs also assist in managing delegated trust models. Some organizations operate their own intermediate CAs under the authority of a root CA. These intermediate CAs often delegate authentication tasks to RAs to distribute workload and improve security. The RA ensures that only verified requests reach the intermediate CA, which then issues the necessary certificates. This layered approach enhances security by adding an additional verification step before certificate issuance.

The importance of RAs is further highlighted in sectors that require strict regulatory compliance, such as finance, healthcare, and government agencies. Regulations such as the General Data Protection Regulation (GDPR), the Health Insurance Portability and Accountability Act (HIPAA), and financial industry standards require strong identity verification and authentication mechanisms to protect sensitive information. RAs help organizations comply with these regulations by ensuring that only verified entities receive digital certificates and that the entire certificate issuance process follows security best practices.

Despite their advantages, RAs must also adhere to strict security policies to prevent misuse. The integrity of an RA is crucial because any compromise could lead to unauthorized certificate issuance, which could undermine trust in the entire PKI system. To mitigate risks, RAs implement multi-factor authentication for administrators, secure communication channels for certificate requests, and audit logs to track all verification activities. Organizations that operate RAs must also ensure that their personnel are properly trained in identity verification processes and adhere to security policies that prevent insider threats.

As digital transformation accelerates, the role of RAs is expanding beyond traditional PKI applications. With the rise of cloud computing, mobile authentication, and the Internet of Things (IoT), RAs are being integrated into automated certificate management systems to support large-scale deployments. In IoT environments, where billions of connected devices require authentication and encryption, RAs help validate device identities before they are issued certificates. This ensures that only trusted devices can communicate within secure networks, preventing unauthorized access and cyberattacks.

Advancements in identity verification technologies are also influencing the evolution of RAs. The use of biometrics, artificial intelligence (AI), and blockchain-based identity management systems is being explored to improve the accuracy and efficiency of identity validation. AI-powered identity verification tools can automate the RA process, reducing manual effort while increasing accuracy in detecting fraudulent certificate requests. Similarly, blockchain-based identity solutions offer a decentralized model for verifying identities without relying solely on traditional CA-based trust hierarchies.

The increasing adoption of remote work, digital banking, and secure online transactions further emphasizes the importance of RAs in protecting digital identities. As organizations continue to rely on digital certificates for authentication, encryption, and document signing, the need for robust identity verification mechanisms remains critical. Whether integrated into enterprise security frameworks, government digital identity programs, or cloud-based authentication services, RAs continue to serve as a cornerstone of trust in digital communications.

Registration Authorities play a crucial role in the PKI ecosystem by verifying identities, managing certificate requests, and enforcing security policies. Their ability to authenticate entities before issuing digital certificates strengthens trust in online interactions and prevents fraudulent use of cryptographic credentials. As cybersecurity threats evolve and digital identities become more interconnected, RAs will remain essential in maintaining secure and reliable digital communications across industries.

The PKI Trust Model

The Public Key Infrastructure (PKI) trust model is the foundation that ensures the security, integrity, and authenticity of digital certificates used for secure communications. Without a well-defined trust model, PKI would not be able to establish confidence in identities, encrypt sensitive data, or verify digital signatures. The trust model defines the relationships between Certificate Authorities (CAs), Registration Authorities (RAs), and end entities, outlining how trust is built, maintained, and propagated within the system. By implementing a structured trust model, PKI enables organizations, governments, and individuals to securely communicate and conduct transactions over the internet.

At the core of the PKI trust model is the concept of hierarchical trust, where trust is established through a chain of digital certificates issued by recognized and trusted authorities. This hierarchy is built on the principle that entities rely on higher-level trusted entities to validate their identities. The highest level of trust resides with root Certificate Authorities (root CAs), which act as the foundation of the PKI system. These root CAs issue certificates to intermediate CAs, which in turn issue certificates to end entities such as websites, organizations, and individuals. This structure forms a trust chain that ensures that all certificates are verifiable back to a trusted root CA.

Trust in PKI is established through digital signatures. When a CA issues a certificate, it signs it with its private key, creating a cryptographic link between the certificate and the CA. Any entity that receives the certificate can verify its authenticity by checking the CA's digital signature using the corresponding public key. This process ensures that the certificate has not been altered and that it was issued by a legitimate CA. If the signature is valid and the CA is trusted, the certificate is accepted. If the signature is invalid or the CA is untrusted, the certificate is rejected, preventing potential security risks.

There are different trust models used in PKI, each designed for specific environments and use cases. The most common model is the hierarchical trust model, also known as the single-root trust model. In this model, a single root CA sits at the top of the hierarchy and issues certificates to subordinate intermediate CAs. These intermediate CAs then issue certificates to end entities. This model is widely used in public PKI systems, such as those that secure websites, online banking, and email encryption. It provides a structured and scalable approach to trust management, ensuring that all certificates can be traced back to a single trusted authority.

Another widely used trust model is the mesh trust model, where multiple CAs trust each other directly without relying on a single root CA. In this decentralized approach, CAs establish cross-certificates that allow them to recognize each other's issued certificates. This model is often used in government and enterprise environments where different organizations need to maintain independent CAs while still recognizing certificates from other trusted entities. The mesh trust model offers flexibility but requires careful management to prevent trust dilution and security risks associated with untrusted certificates.

The bridge trust model is another approach used in large-scale environments where multiple organizations operate independent PKI systems. Instead of requiring direct trust relationships between all CAs, a central bridge CA acts as an intermediary that connects different PKI domains. This model is commonly used in government and military applications, where different agencies need to establish trust without merging their PKI systems. The bridge trust model enables interoperability between separate PKI environments while maintaining control over trust relationships.

A less common but important model is the web-of-trust model, which does not rely on a centralized CA hierarchy. Instead, trust is established directly between users through mutual verification and endorsement. This model is commonly used in decentralized environments, such as Pretty Good Privacy (PGP) encryption, where individuals sign each other's public keys to create a distributed trust network. While the web-of-trust model provides flexibility and resilience against CA compromises, it lacks the scalability and structured validation process of traditional CA-based PKI models.

The effectiveness of the PKI trust model depends on proper certificate validation and revocation mechanisms. When a certificate is presented for authentication, the receiving system must verify its validity by checking the certificate chain, ensuring that each CA in the chain is trusted. This process is known as certificate path validation and is critical for preventing the acceptance of fraudulent or tampered certificates.

Certificate revocation is also a crucial aspect of the trust model. If a certificate's private key is compromised, or if an entity is no longer trustworthy, the certificate must be revoked to prevent its continued use. CAs maintain Certificate Revocation Lists (CRLs) and provide Online Certificate Status Protocol (OCSP) services to allow entities to check whether a certificate is still valid. Without proper revocation mechanisms, a compromised certificate could be used for malicious purposes, such as phishing attacks or unauthorized data decryption.

PKI trust models must also address security risks associated with compromised or malicious CAs. If a CA is compromised, attackers can issue fraudulent certificates that appear legitimate. To mitigate this risk, browsers, operating systems, and security frameworks maintain a list of trusted CAs and regularly update it based on security incidents. In cases where a CA is found to be issuing fraudulent certificates, it can be distrusted by removing it from trusted root certificate stores, effectively invalidating all certificates issued by that CA.

The continuous evolution of cyber threats and cryptographic advancements necessitates ongoing improvements to PKI trust models. The rise of quantum computing presents a potential challenge to traditional cryptographic algorithms used in PKI, prompting research into post-quantum cryptography to develop quantum-resistant trust mechanisms. Additionally, blockchain technology is being explored as a potential alternative to traditional CA-based trust models, offering decentralized and tamper-proof ways to manage digital identities.

The PKI trust model provides the foundation for digital security by ensuring that entities can trust the authenticity and validity of digital certificates. Whether implemented in hierarchical, mesh, bridge, or web-of-trust models, PKI enables secure communications, authentication, and data protection. As technology and security threats continue to evolve, maintaining a robust and adaptable PKI trust model remains essential for ensuring trust and integrity in digital interactions.

Root and Intermediate Certificate Authorities

Certificate Authorities (CAs) are the backbone of Public Key Infrastructure (PKI), responsible for issuing and managing digital certificates that enable secure communication, authentication, and data integrity. Within the CA hierarchy, there are two main types of CAs: root Certificate Authorities and intermediate Certificate

Authorities. Understanding the roles, responsibilities, and relationships between these entities is crucial for maintaining trust in PKI systems.

A root Certificate Authority is the highest authority in the trust hierarchy. It is responsible for issuing certificates to subordinate CAs, known as intermediate CAs, which in turn issue certificates to end entities such as websites, organizations, and individuals. The root CA's certificate is self-signed, meaning it does not rely on any higher authority for validation. Because root CAs are the ultimate source of trust, their private keys must be kept extremely secure. If a root CA is compromised, every certificate issued within its chain of trust is rendered invalid, leading to widespread security vulnerabilities.

To mitigate risks associated with root CA compromise, best practices dictate that root CAs should be kept offline and used only when necessary, such as signing new intermediate CA certificates. This offline operation, also known as an air-gapped root CA, ensures that the private key of the root CA is not exposed to potential cyber threats. Since root CAs play a foundational role in establishing trust, their security policies and procedures must be extremely strict, including physical security measures, access controls, and regular audits.

Because root CAs are too valuable to be used for direct certificate issuance to end users, they delegate the responsibility of certificate issuance to intermediate Certificate Authorities. An intermediate CA is a subordinate CA that receives its certificate from the root CA and is authorized to issue certificates to lower-level CAs or end entities. This hierarchical model ensures that the root CA remains protected while allowing scalability and flexibility in certificate issuance.

The use of intermediate CAs provides an additional layer of security and compartmentalization. If an intermediate CA is compromised, only the certificates issued by that specific intermediate CA are affected, while the root CA and other intermediate CAs remain secure. This limits the scope of damage and allows organizations to revoke and replace compromised certificates without undermining the entire trust infrastructure. For this reason, organizations often implement multiple intermediate CAs for different functions, such as one for issuing

SSL/TLS certificates, another for email encryption, and another for internal authentication.

One of the key functions of intermediate CAs is certificate lifecycle management. This includes issuing new certificates, renewing expiring certificates, and revoking certificates that are no longer valid or have been compromised. When an intermediate CA revokes a certificate, it updates the Certificate Revocation List (CRL) or provides real-time status verification through the Online Certificate Status Protocol (OCSP). These mechanisms allow systems to check whether a certificate is still trustworthy before accepting it for secure communication.

Intermediate CAs also play a role in compliance and policy enforcement. Many industries and regulatory bodies require strict adherence to security policies when issuing and managing digital certificates. Intermediate CAs are configured to follow these policies, ensuring that only properly validated entities receive certificates. This is particularly important in financial institutions, government agencies, and healthcare organizations, where trust and security are paramount.

In some PKI architectures, organizations may operate their own private intermediate CAs under a public root CA. This approach is commonly used by large enterprises that need to issue internal certificates for employees, servers, and devices while maintaining trust in a public PKI system. By running their own intermediate CAs, organizations gain greater control over certificate issuance while leveraging the trust of an established root CA. This model is often seen in hybrid environments where private and public trust coexist.

Another key consideration in managing root and intermediate CAs is certificate expiration and renewal. Root CA certificates typically have long lifespans, often 20 to 30 years, because replacing them is a complex and disruptive process. Intermediate CAs, on the other hand, have shorter validity periods, typically ranging from 5 to 10 years. This shorter lifespan ensures that if an intermediate CA's private key is compromised, the risk is limited to a shorter timeframe. When an intermediate CA certificate nears expiration, it must be renewed by the root CA or replaced with a new intermediate CA to maintain continuous trust.

Security breaches involving root or intermediate CAs have had significant consequences in the past. When a CA is compromised or found to have issued fraudulent certificates, browsers and operating systems may distrust the CA by removing its root certificate from their trust stores. This effectively invalidates all certificates issued under that CA, disrupting secure communications for affected entities. To prevent such incidents, CAs must implement stringent security measures, such as hardware security modules (HSMs) to protect private keys, multi-factor authentication for administrative access, and continuous monitoring for suspicious activity.

The evolution of PKI has also introduced new models for CA management, including cloud-based CA services and decentralized trust mechanisms. Cloud-based CAs offer scalable certificate issuance and management solutions while maintaining the security of root and intermediate CAs in dedicated data centers. Meanwhile, decentralized models, such as blockchain-based identity verification systems, seek to reduce reliance on traditional hierarchical CA structures by distributing trust across a network of independent entities.

Despite new innovations, the traditional root-intermediate-end entity trust model remains the foundation of modern PKI. By carefully managing root and intermediate CAs, organizations and certificate authorities can ensure that digital certificates remain secure, trustworthy, and resilient against evolving cybersecurity threats. The hierarchical structure of PKI, with clear separation between root and intermediate CAs, continues to provide a scalable and secure approach to digital trust.

Certificate Lifecycle Management

Certificate lifecycle management is a crucial aspect of Public Key Infrastructure (PKI), ensuring that digital certificates are properly issued, maintained, renewed, and revoked when necessary. Digital certificates play a fundamental role in securing communications, authenticating identities, and protecting sensitive data. However, without effective lifecycle management, organizations face security risks such as expired certificates, unrevoked compromised keys, and unauthorized access to critical systems. A well-structured certificate lifecycle management process ensures continuous security and compliance while preventing disruptions in digital operations.

The lifecycle of a digital certificate begins with the certificate request process. When an entity, such as a website, server, or user, requires a certificate, it must first generate a key pair consisting of a public key and a private key. The public key is included in a Certificate Signing Request (CSR), which is sent to a Certificate Authority (CA) for validation. The CSR also contains identifying information, such as the domain name, organization details, and intended certificate usage. The CA verifies the identity of the requester and, upon approval, issues a signed certificate that binds the public key to the entity's identity.

Once issued, the certificate enters the active phase, where it is used to secure communications and authenticate entities. During this period, it is crucial to monitor the certificate to ensure that it remains valid and functional. Proper monitoring includes tracking expiration dates, checking for security vulnerabilities, and ensuring compliance with cryptographic best practices. Organizations often deploy certificate management tools to automate tracking and renewal processes, preventing unexpected failures caused by expired certificates.

One of the major challenges in certificate lifecycle management is the expiration of certificates. Every certificate has a predefined validity period, typically ranging from one to three years for publicly trusted certificates and up to ten years for certain private certificates. When a certificate reaches its expiration date, it is no longer considered valid, and systems relying on it may refuse connections or display security warnings. To avoid disruptions, certificates must be renewed before they expire.

The renewal process involves requesting a new certificate from the CA before the current one expires. In most cases, the renewal process is similar to the initial request, where a new CSR is generated, and the CA revalidates the entity's identity. Many organizations implement automated certificate renewal systems that proactively request and deploy new certificates, reducing the risk of service outages due to expired certificates.

Beyond expiration and renewal, certificate revocation is another critical aspect of lifecycle management. A certificate may need to be revoked before its expiration if it is compromised, misused, or no longer needed. Common reasons for revocation include private key compromise, employee or domain ownership changes, and policy violations. When a certificate is revoked, the CA updates its Certificate Revocation List (CRL) or uses the Online Certificate Status Protocol (OCSP) to inform users and systems that the certificate is no longer trusted.

While CRLs provide a list of revoked certificates, they must be regularly downloaded and updated, which can cause delays. OCSP, on the other hand, allows real-time certificate status verification, improving efficiency and security. Many modern PKI implementations rely on OCSP stapling, which reduces the burden on clients by having the server periodically fetch its revocation status and present it during TLS handshakes.

As organizations grow and rely on thousands of certificates across various systems, certificate inventory management becomes essential. A lack of visibility into active certificates can lead to untracked expirations, unrevoked compromised certificates, and security vulnerabilities. Certificate management platforms help organizations maintain a centralized inventory of all issued certificates, track their status, and enforce policies to ensure secure certificate usage.

In enterprise environments, managing certificates manually is inefficient and prone to errors. To address this, organizations implement certificate automation solutions, such as Automated Certificate Management Environments (ACME), which streamline the issuance, renewal, and deployment of certificates. ACME, widely used in services like Let's Encrypt, allows servers to automatically request and install certificates without human intervention, significantly improving security and operational efficiency.

Security policies surrounding certificate lifecycle management must also address key management. Since digital certificates rely on cryptographic key pairs, protecting private keys is crucial. If a private key is compromised, attackers can impersonate the entity associated with the certificate, leading to security breaches. To prevent such risks, organizations store private keys in Hardware Security Modules (HSMs) or secure key vaults that enforce strict access controls and encryption mechanisms.

In addition to security best practices, regulatory compliance is a driving factor in certificate lifecycle management. Industries such as finance, healthcare, and government must adhere to stringent security frameworks that require proper handling of certificates. Compliance standards like the General Data Protection Regulation (GDPR), Payment Card Industry Data Security Standard (PCI DSS), and Federal Information Security Management Act (FISMA) mandate secure certificate issuance, revocation, and renewal procedures. Organizations that fail to comply with these standards risk penalties and security vulnerabilities.

As technology evolves, new challenges in certificate lifecycle management continue to emerge. The rise of quantum computing poses a potential threat to traditional encryption algorithms, prompting research into quantum-resistant cryptography. Organizations must stay ahead by adopting cryptographic agility strategies, ensuring they can transition to new encryption standards when needed.

Additionally, the shift toward cloud computing and hybrid infrastructures requires new approaches to managing certificates across distributed environments. Traditional on-premise PKI solutions may not be sufficient for cloud-native applications, leading to increased adoption of cloud-based certificate management services. These solutions provide centralized visibility, automation, and security controls, allowing organizations to scale certificate management across diverse infrastructures.

Certificate lifecycle management is a continuous process that requires careful oversight and automation to ensure security, reliability, and compliance. Organizations that implement effective certificate management strategies can prevent service disruptions, mitigate security risks, and maintain trust in their digital communications. By leveraging automation, monitoring tools, and best practices, enterprises can ensure that their certificates remain valid, properly renewed, and revoked when necessary, reducing vulnerabilities and enhancing overall cybersecurity resilience.

Certificate Revocation: CRL and OCSP

Certificate revocation is a crucial aspect of Public Key Infrastructure (PKI) that ensures compromised, expired, or untrustworthy digital certificates can no longer be used for authentication, encryption, or secure communication. Digital certificates provide trust by binding a public key to an entity's identity, but if a certificate becomes invalid before its expiration date, it must be revoked to prevent misuse. Without an effective revocation mechanism, malicious actors could exploit revoked certificates to impersonate legitimate entities, intercept communications, or execute fraudulent activities. The two primary methods used for certificate revocation are the Certificate Revocation List (CRL) and the Online Certificate Status Protocol (OCSP). Both approaches serve the same purpose—informing users and systems that a certificate should no longer be trusted—but they operate in different ways and have distinct advantages and limitations.

A Certificate Revocation List (CRL) is a digitally signed list of revoked certificates maintained and published by a Certificate Authority (CA). When a certificate is revoked, its serial number is added to the CRL, which is periodically updated and distributed to systems that rely on certificate validation. The CRL allows entities to verify whether a certificate is still valid before establishing a secure connection or trusting a digital signature. However, since CRLs are updated at set intervals, there can be a delay between the time a certificate is revoked and when it is recognized as revoked by systems relying on the CRL. This delay creates a security risk, especially in cases where immediate revocation is necessary due to private key compromise or fraudulent activity.

CRLs are structured based on the X.509 certificate standard, which defines how certificate information is formatted and managed. Each CRL includes a header containing metadata, such as the issuing CA's identity, the date the CRL was generated, and the next scheduled update. Following the header is the list of revoked certificate serial numbers, along with the revocation reason code and the revocation date. Common revocation reasons include key compromise, CA compromise, cessation of operation, and certificate supersession. These reasons help relying parties understand why a certificate has been revoked and assess the potential security implications.

One of the challenges with CRLs is their size and distribution. As more certificates are revoked, the CRL grows larger, increasing the bandwidth and processing power required to download and verify the list. In large PKI environments, CRLs can become unwieldy, leading to delays in revocation checks. To address this, organizations implement delta CRLs, which contain only the recently revoked certificates since the last full CRL update. This reduces the overhead of downloading a complete CRL while still keeping certificate validation up to date.

While CRLs provide a static list of revoked certificates, the Online Certificate Status Protocol (OCSP) offers a more dynamic and efficient approach to certificate validation. OCSP allows clients to query a CA's OCSP responder in real time to check the status of a specific certificate. Instead of downloading a full CRL, a client sends a request containing the certificate's serial number, and the OCSP responder replies with the certificate's status: good, revoked, or unknown. This real-time validation ensures that certificates are checked against the most up-to-date revocation information, reducing the risks associated with delayed CRL updates.

One of the key benefits of OCSP is its lightweight nature compared to CRLs. Since clients only request the status of a single certificate at a time, OCSP minimizes network bandwidth usage and reduces the computational overhead of processing large revocation lists. This makes OCSP particularly advantageous for environments requiring frequent certificate validation, such as secure web browsing, email encryption, and financial transactions.

However, OCSP also has its own limitations. Because it requires an online connection to an OCSP responder, certificate validation can be affected by network latency or service availability issues. If the OCSP responder is unreachable, clients may be unable to determine the revocation status of a certificate, leading to potential security risks. To mitigate this, many systems implement OCSP stapling, an optimization that reduces reliance on direct OCSP queries.

OCSP stapling enhances performance and security by allowing the certificate holder (such as a web server) to retrieve and cache a signed OCSP response from the CA's OCSP responder. The server then "staples" this response to its TLS handshake when communicating with clients. This means that clients do not need to contact the OCSP responder directly, reducing latency and improving privacy by preventing third parties from tracking which certificates are being validated. OCSP stapling is widely used in HTTPS connections to improve efficiency while maintaining strong security.

Despite their differences, both CRLs and OCSP are essential for managing certificate revocation. Many PKI implementations use a combination of both methods to balance security and performance. CRLs provide a comprehensive backup mechanism for checking revocation status when OCSP is unavailable, while OCSP enables real-time validation to prevent security gaps. Organizations deploying PKI must carefully choose the appropriate revocation strategy based on their security requirements, infrastructure limitations, and regulatory compliance obligations.

Regulatory frameworks and security standards mandate proper certificate revocation management to ensure trust in digital transactions. Compliance standards such as the General Data Protection Regulation (GDPR), Payment Card Industry Data Security Standard (PCI DSS), and Federal Information Processing Standards (FIPS 140-2) require organizations to implement effective revocation mechanisms to prevent the misuse of expired or compromised certificates. Failure to revoke untrusted certificates can lead to data breaches, fraud, and reputational damage.

As PKI continues to evolve, new technologies and improvements to revocation mechanisms are being explored. Emerging cryptographic techniques, such as blockchain-based revocation tracking, aim to create decentralized and tamper-proof revocation systems that eliminate reliance on centralized CAs. Additionally, advancements in post-quantum cryptography may introduce new revocation challenges, requiring updated protocols to ensure certificate trust in the post-quantum era.

Proper certificate revocation management is a critical aspect of maintaining digital trust. Organizations must implement a robust revocation strategy that combines CRLs, OCSP, and automation to ensure timely and reliable certificate validation. By leveraging best practices, including OCSP stapling, delta CRLs, and automated monitoring, PKI systems can effectively mitigate risks associated with compromised or expired certificates while ensuring secure digital communications.

X.509 Certificate Standard

The X.509 certificate standard is the foundation of modern Public Key Infrastructure (PKI), providing a universally recognized format for digital certificates. These certificates are used to establish trust in secure communications, authenticate entities, and enable encryption for sensitive data transmission. X.509 defines the structure and attributes of digital certificates, ensuring interoperability between different systems and applications. Without this standard, the secure exchange of information over the internet, including HTTPS connections, email encryption, and digital signatures, would not be possible.

Developed by the International Telecommunication Union (ITU-T), the X.509 standard was first introduced in 1988 as part of the X.500 directory services framework. Over time, it has evolved to support various security applications and cryptographic protocols, adapting to the growing needs of cybersecurity. X.509 certificates are widely used in SSL/TLS encryption, secure email (S/MIME), code signing, and identity management systems. They play a critical role in establishing trust by binding an entity's public key to its identity, ensuring that only legitimate parties can access encrypted communications or sign digital documents.

An X.509 certificate contains structured information in a standardized format, enabling systems to verify the authenticity of the certificate and the entity it represents. The core components of an X.509 certificate include the certificate version, serial number, signature algorithm, issuer information, validity period, subject information, public key, extensions, and the digital signature of the issuing

Certificate Authority (CA). Each field serves a specific purpose in establishing trust and ensuring security in digital transactions.

The version number indicates the format of the certificate and the features it supports. The most commonly used versions are X.509 v3, which introduces extensions that allow for enhanced functionality, including key usage restrictions, alternative subject names, and certificate policies. These extensions enable organizations to customize certificates based on their security needs and regulatory requirements.

The serial number is a unique identifier assigned by the issuing CA. This number helps differentiate certificates and is crucial for revocation tracking. If a certificate is found to be compromised or no longer valid, its serial number is added to a Certificate Revocation List (CRL) or checked against an Online Certificate Status Protocol (OCSP) responder.

The signature algorithm specifies the cryptographic algorithm used to sign the certificate. This ensures the integrity of the certificate and prevents tampering. Commonly used signature algorithms include RSA with SHA-256, ECDSA with SHA-384, and other hash-based cryptographic functions that provide strong security guarantees.

The issuer information identifies the CA that issued the certificate. It includes details such as the CA's common name, organization, and country. This information allows relying parties to trace the certificate back to a trusted CA and verify its authenticity.

The validity period defines the start and expiration dates of the certificate. Certificates have a limited lifespan, typically ranging from one to three years for public certificates and longer for internal certificates. Expired certificates must be renewed or replaced to maintain security and prevent service disruptions. The validity period ensures that certificates are periodically updated with stronger encryption algorithms if needed.

The subject information identifies the entity associated with the certificate. For website certificates, this is typically the domain name, while for personal or organizational certificates, it may include the individual's name, company details, or email address. The subject field plays a crucial role in authentication, ensuring that the certificate is issued to the correct entity.

The public key is the cryptographic key associated with the certificate holder. This key is used for encryption and verification purposes, ensuring that only the corresponding private key holder can decrypt or sign data. The strength of the public key depends on the algorithm and key length used, with RSA (2048-bit or higher), Elliptic Curve Cryptography (ECC), and post-quantum cryptography being among the commonly used methods.

X.509 v3 certificates introduce extensions, which provide additional information about the certificate's usage and constraints. Some of the most important extensions include the Key Usage extension, which specifies whether the certificate can be used for digital signatures, key encipherment, or certificate signing. The Extended Key Usage extension further refines the allowed functions, distinguishing between TLS authentication, email protection, code signing, and other applications. The Subject Alternative Name (SAN) extension allows a certificate to support multiple domain names or IP addresses, making it particularly useful for multi-domain SSL/TLS certificates.

The Authority Key Identifier (AKI) and Subject Key Identifier (SKI) extensions help with certificate chain validation. The AKI links a certificate to its issuing CA, ensuring that it is correctly associated with a trusted root or intermediate certificate. The SKI uniquely identifies a certificate's key pair, aiding in efficient certificate management and validation.

Finally, the digital signature of the issuing CA provides cryptographic proof that the certificate was issued by a trusted authority. This signature is generated using the CA's private key and can be verified using its corresponding public key. If the signature is valid and the CA is trusted, the certificate is accepted. If the signature is invalid or the CA is untrusted, the certificate is rejected, preventing unauthorized entities from impersonating legitimate organizations.

X.509 certificates are fundamental to PKI, enabling secure communication across various industries and applications. In web security, they ensure that users connect to legitimate HTTPS websites, protecting against phishing attacks and man-in-the-middle threats. In enterprise environments, they facilitate secure authentication through smart cards, VPN access, and identity federation systems. In software security, they verify the authenticity of digitally signed applications, preventing malware distribution.

Despite their widespread adoption, X.509 certificates must be managed properly to maintain security. Organizations must implement certificate lifecycle management processes, including renewal, revocation, and automation to prevent expired or compromised certificates from causing security incidents. Certificate transparency logs and automated monitoring tools help detect fraudulent or misissued certificates, enhancing trust in PKI ecosystems.

As cybersecurity threats evolve, the X.509 standard continues to adapt to new challenges. The rise of quantum computing presents a potential risk to traditional cryptographic algorithms used in X.509 certificates, prompting research into quantum-resistant alternatives. Additionally, decentralized identity systems and blockchain-based PKI models are emerging as potential alternatives to traditional certificate-based trust mechanisms.

The X.509 certificate standard remains the backbone of digital trust, ensuring the authenticity, integrity, and confidentiality of communications across the internet and enterprise systems. Its structured format, extensibility, and integration with PKI make it an indispensable tool for securing modern digital interactions. As technology advances, continuous improvements to the X.509 framework will be essential in maintaining secure and trusted communications in an increasingly interconnected world.

Key Generation and Key Management

Key generation and key management are critical components of Public Key Infrastructure (PKI) and cryptographic security. The strength of encryption, authentication, and digital signatures relies on the secure creation, storage, distribution, and protection of cryptographic keys. If keys are not properly managed, even the most advanced encryption algorithms can be rendered useless, exposing sensitive information to potential attacks. Proper key management ensures the confidentiality, integrity, and availability of cryptographic keys throughout their lifecycle.

Key generation is the first step in cryptographic security. A cryptographic key is a random sequence of bits used in encryption and decryption processes. The security of the key depends on its randomness, length, and the cryptographic algorithm used. Weak or predictable keys can be easily guessed or cracked, compromising the entire security system. Therefore, key generation must follow strict cryptographic standards to ensure resistance against brute-force attacks and other cryptanalytic techniques.

There are two main types of cryptographic keys: symmetric keys and asymmetric key pairs. Symmetric keys are used in encryption algorithms such as Advanced Encryption Standard (AES) and Data Encryption Standard (DES), where the same key is used for both encryption and decryption. These keys must be kept secret and securely shared between communicating parties. Because symmetric encryption relies on a single key, key distribution is a major challenge, as unauthorized access to the key can compromise encrypted data.

Asymmetric key pairs, used in public-key cryptography, consist of a public key and a private key. The public key is shared openly, allowing anyone to encrypt data, while the private key is kept secret and used for decryption. Algorithms such as Rivest-Shamir-Adleman (RSA) and Elliptic Curve Cryptography (ECC) rely on this key pair mechanism to secure communications and authenticate identities. The security of asymmetric encryption depends on the mathematical difficulty of deriving the private key from the public key, making it a more secure option for key exchange and digital signatures.

Once cryptographic keys are generated, they must be securely stored and managed to prevent unauthorized access or loss. Key management includes processes such as key storage, key distribution, key rotation, key revocation, and key destruction. Poor key management can lead to security vulnerabilities, including stolen encryption keys, expired certificates, and compromised authentication systems. Organizations implement Key Management Systems (KMS) and Hardware Security

Modules (HSMs) to protect cryptographic keys and enforce strict security policies.

Key storage is one of the most important aspects of key management. Private keys should never be stored in plaintext or in easily accessible locations, such as application code, configuration files, or databases without encryption. Instead, private keys should be stored in secure environments, such as HSMs, which are specialized hardware devices designed to generate, store, and manage cryptographic keys securely. HSMs provide physical and logical protection, ensuring that keys are never exposed to unauthorized users or malware.

In cloud-based environments, organizations use Cloud Key Management Services (CKMS) to store and manage cryptographic keys securely. These services provide encryption, key rotation, and access control mechanisms to ensure that cloud-based applications and storage solutions remain protected. Cloud-based key management solutions integrate with major cloud platforms, allowing enterprises to manage their encryption keys across distributed systems while maintaining compliance with security regulations.

Key distribution is another critical challenge in key management. For symmetric encryption, securely sharing the key between communicating parties without exposing it to potential attackers is a major concern. Organizations use secure key exchange protocols, such as the Diffie-Hellman key exchange or Elliptic Curve Diffie-Hellman (ECDH), to establish a shared secret key over an insecure network. These protocols allow parties to generate a shared encryption key without transmitting the key itself, reducing the risk of interception.

For asymmetric encryption, key distribution is more straightforward, as the public key can be shared openly without compromising security. However, ensuring the authenticity of public keys is crucial. If an attacker replaces a legitimate public key with a malicious one, they can intercept and decrypt messages intended for the legitimate recipient. To prevent this, organizations use Public Key Infrastructure (PKI), where trusted Certificate Authorities (CAs) verify and issue digital certificates that bind public keys to their rightful owners.

Key rotation and key expiration policies help minimize security risks by ensuring that cryptographic keys are not used indefinitely. Over time, keys may become vulnerable due to advances in computing power or cryptographic attacks. Regular key rotation ensures that old keys are replaced with new ones before they become a security risk. Organizations implement automated key rotation processes, where encryption keys are periodically changed without disrupting operations. This practice is particularly important in industries that handle sensitive financial or personal data, such as banking, healthcare, and government services.

Key revocation is necessary when a cryptographic key is compromised, suspected to be at risk, or no longer needed. If a private key is exposed, it must be revoked immediately to prevent unauthorized access. In PKI, Certificate Revocation Lists (CRLs) and Online Certificate Status Protocol (OCSP) are used to notify users and systems that a certificate associated with a compromised key is no longer trusted. Effective key revocation mechanisms prevent attackers from exploiting stolen or outdated cryptographic keys.

Key destruction is the final phase in the lifecycle of a cryptographic key. When a key is no longer needed, it must be securely deleted to prevent unauthorized recovery. Secure key destruction methods include overwriting, cryptographic erasure, and physical destruction of hardware containing the key. Simply deleting a key from a system is not sufficient, as remnants of the key may still be recoverable using forensic techniques. Proper key destruction ensures that retired cryptographic keys cannot be misused or recovered by malicious actors.

Regulatory compliance plays a significant role in key management. Security frameworks such as the General Data Protection Regulation (GDPR), Payment Card Industry Data Security Standard (PCI DSS), and National Institute of Standards and Technology (NIST) guidelines require organizations to implement strict key management policies. Compliance ensures that cryptographic keys are generated, stored, and managed in a way that protects sensitive information and prevents data breaches. Organizations that fail to comply with these standards may face financial penalties and reputational damage.

As cybersecurity threats continue to evolve, the importance of key management increases. The rise of quantum computing presents new challenges for traditional cryptographic algorithms, prompting research into post-quantum cryptography. Organizations must stay ahead by adopting cryptographic agility strategies, ensuring that they can transition to new encryption standards when necessary. Emerging technologies such as blockchain-based key management and zero-trust architectures further enhance key security by reducing reliance on centralized key storage and improving access control mechanisms.

Proper key generation and management are essential for maintaining the security and integrity of encrypted communications, authentication mechanisms, and digital transactions. Organizations that implement best practices in key lifecycle management can mitigate risks, protect sensitive data, and ensure compliance with security regulations. As encryption technologies advance, robust key management will continue to be a fundamental aspect of cybersecurity, safeguarding digital assets in an increasingly connected world.

Secure Key Storage and Hardware Security Modules (HSMs)

Secure key storage is one of the most critical aspects of cryptographic security. Cryptographic keys are the foundation of encryption, authentication, and digital signatures, making them highly valuable targets for attackers. If an encryption key is exposed or stolen, even the strongest cryptographic algorithms become useless, as an attacker can decrypt sensitive data, forge digital signatures, or impersonate legitimate users. Therefore, organizations must implement strong key storage mechanisms to protect private keys from unauthorized access, theft, or corruption.

The primary goal of secure key storage is to ensure that cryptographic keys remain confidential and accessible only to authorized entities. Keys must be protected from software vulnerabilities, insider threats, and hardware attacks. Several methods exist for storing keys securely, ranging from software-based approaches to specialized hardware devices designed for cryptographic security. The level of security required depends on the sensitivity of the data being protected and the threat model of the organization.

Software-based key storage solutions include secure key vaults, encrypted key files, and cloud-based key management services. Secure key vaults are software applications designed to store and manage cryptographic keys securely. These vaults use strong encryption and access control mechanisms to prevent unauthorized retrieval of keys. Examples of software-based key vaults include HashiCorp Vault, AWS Key Management Service (KMS), and Microsoft Azure Key Vault.

While software-based solutions offer convenience and flexibility, they are vulnerable to attacks such as memory dumping, malware, and privilege escalation exploits. If an attacker gains access to the system running the key vault, they may be able to extract encryption keys from memory or disk storage. To mitigate these risks, organizations implement strict access control policies, multi-factor authentication, and hardware-backed encryption to protect keys stored in software environments.

For higher levels of security, organizations use Hardware Security Modules (HSMs), which are dedicated hardware devices designed for cryptographic key storage and operations. HSMs provide a secure, tamper-resistant environment for generating, storing, and using cryptographic keys, significantly reducing the risk of key exposure. These devices are widely used in enterprise environments, financial institutions, and government agencies where cryptographic security is a top priority.

An HSM is a specialized piece of hardware equipped with secure processors, physical security mechanisms, and built-in cryptographic functions. Unlike software-based key storage, where keys can be extracted if the system is compromised, HSMs are designed to prevent unauthorized access even if an attacker has physical possession of the device. Many HSMs include tamper-evident and tamper-resistant features that detect and respond to attempts at physical intrusion. If an unauthorized attempt to access the HSM is detected, the device may erase its stored keys automatically to prevent compromise.

HSMs provide a variety of cryptographic functions, including key generation, encryption, decryption, digital signatures, and certificate management. These operations are performed entirely within the HSM, ensuring that private keys are never exposed outside the secure hardware environment. This architecture significantly reduces the risk of key theft, as even privileged users or administrators cannot extract keys from the device.

One of the key advantages of using HSMs is their ability to support strong key management policies. Organizations can define strict policies for key access, including multi-factor authentication, role-based access control, and hardware-backed encryption. Many HSMs also support secure key backup and recovery, ensuring that cryptographic keys remain available even in the event of hardware failure.

There are different types of HSMs designed for various use cases. Network-attached HSMs are standalone appliances that connect to enterprise networks, allowing multiple systems to securely access cryptographic services. These HSMs are often deployed in data centers to provide centralized key management and encryption services for an organization's infrastructure. PCIe HSMs are hardware modules that can be installed directly into servers, providing high-speed cryptographic processing for applications such as SSL/TLS encryption, digital signatures, and database encryption.

Cloud-based HSM solutions have also emerged, offering the security benefits of traditional HSMs with the flexibility of cloud computing. Cloud HSMs are managed HSM services provided by cloud vendors, such as AWS CloudHSM and Google Cloud HSM. These solutions allow organizations to securely generate and store encryption keys while leveraging cloud scalability and high availability. Cloud HSMs integrate with cloud-native security services, enabling businesses to protect their data without managing on-premises hardware.

HSMs play a critical role in securing Public Key Infrastructure (PKI) by protecting the private keys of Certificate Authorities (CAs). Since the security of PKI depends on the trustworthiness of private keys, CAs use HSMs to securely store and manage root and intermediate CA keys. This prevents key compromise and unauthorized certificate issuance, ensuring the integrity of digital certificates used for authentication, encryption, and digital signatures.

The use of HSMs extends beyond PKI and enterprise encryption. Financial institutions rely on HSMs to secure payment transactions and protect sensitive customer data. In the payment industry, HSMs are used to encrypt credit card transactions, generate PIN codes, and secure online banking authentication systems. The Payment Card Industry Data Security Standard (PCI DSS) mandates the use of HSMs for secure cryptographic processing in financial services, ensuring compliance with industry security standards.

Despite their security benefits, HSMs also present challenges in terms of cost, management complexity, and integration with existing infrastructure. Traditional HSMs require significant investment in hardware, maintenance, and operational expertise. Organizations must carefully evaluate their security needs and regulatory requirements before deploying HSM solutions. For businesses that require strong encryption but lack the resources to manage dedicated HSMs, cloud-based HSM services provide a viable alternative.

The evolution of cryptographic security continues to influence the development of HSMs and secure key storage technologies. With the rise of quantum computing, traditional cryptographic algorithms may become vulnerable, prompting research into quantum-resistant encryption methods. Future HSMs will need to support post-quantum cryptography (PQC) to protect against emerging threats. Additionally, advances in zero-trust architectures and confidential computing are driving new approaches to securing cryptographic keys in modern computing environments.

Organizations that implement robust key storage solutions, whether through HSMs, cloud-based services, or secure key vaults, can significantly enhance their security posture. Protecting cryptographic keys is essential for maintaining data confidentiality, preventing identity theft, and ensuring the integrity of digital transactions. By integrating secure key storage best practices with strong access controls, monitoring, and encryption policies, businesses can safeguard their cryptographic assets against evolving cybersecurity threats.

Certificate Policies and Practice Statements

Certificate Policies (CPs) and Certification Practice Statements (CPSs) are essential documents in Public Key Infrastructure (PKI) that define the rules, procedures, and security requirements governing the issuance, management, and use of digital certificates. These documents establish the foundation for trust in PKI by ensuring that Certificate Authorities (CAs) operate in a secure, transparent, and standardized manner. Without well-defined CPs and CPSs, there would be no formal framework to ensure that digital certificates are issued and managed consistently, leading to potential security risks and trust failures in online communications and transactions.

A Certificate Policy (CP) is a high-level document that defines the overall policies and security requirements that a CA must follow when issuing certificates. It serves as a broad framework that outlines the intended use cases of the certificates, the level of assurance provided, and the responsibilities of various entities involved in PKI. A CP provides guidance on the types of certificates issued, the validation procedures required, and the security measures implemented to protect the certificate issuance process.

Certificate Policies are designed to meet the needs of different industries and regulatory requirements. For example, a government agency may require stricter identity verification processes for digital identity certificates, while an e-commerce website may prioritize SSL/TLS certificates for encrypting web traffic. By defining these policies, organizations ensure that certificates meet the security standards necessary for their intended use.

The Certification Practice Statement (CPS) is a more detailed technical document that describes how a CA implements the policies outlined in the CP. While the CP defines "what" needs to be done, the CPS specifies "how" it is done. The CPS details the operational procedures of the CA, including certificate issuance, validation, revocation, and security controls. It provides a comprehensive description of the technical and procedural steps followed to ensure compliance with the CP.

A CPS includes specific information about the CA's infrastructure, cryptographic practices, personnel responsibilities, and risk management strategies. It defines how the CA generates key pairs, how certificate requests are validated, how certificates are revoked, and how audit logs are maintained. This level of detail ensures that the CA operates securely and transparently, reducing the risk of fraud or improper certificate issuance.

One of the primary components of a CP is the definition of certificate types and assurance levels. Different certificates provide different levels of trust, and the CP specifies how each type of certificate should be used. For example, a CP may define three levels of assurance:

Domain Validation (DV) Certificates: Issued with minimal verification, often used for encrypting web traffic without verifying the organization's identity.

Organization Validation (OV) Certificates: Require additional verification of the organization's legal existence and identity.

Extended Validation (EV) Certificates: Offer the highest level of assurance, requiring rigorous identity verification before issuance.

The CP also defines the roles and responsibilities of various PKI participants, including CAs, Registration Authorities (RAs), and certificate subscribers. CAs are responsible for issuing and managing certificates according to the CP's security guidelines. RAs handle the verification of certificate requests, ensuring that applicants meet the necessary requirements before a certificate is issued. Certificate subscribers, such as businesses or individuals using digital certificates, must follow security best practices to protect their private keys and report any security incidents to the CA.

In addition to certificate issuance, the CP and CPS outline the procedures for certificate revocation and lifecycle management. If a certificate's private key is compromised, the CA must follow strict revocation procedures to ensure that the compromised certificate is no longer trusted. The CP defines acceptable reasons for revocation, such as key compromise, organizational changes, or policy violations. The CPS provides technical details on how revocation is handled, including the use of Certificate Revocation Lists (CRLs) and the Online Certificate Status Protocol (OCSP) for real-time status verification.

Security controls are another critical aspect of CPs and CPSs. A CP specifies the minimum security requirements that a CA must implement, including physical security, personnel training, and cryptographic key protection. The CPS provides detailed descriptions of these security measures, such as multi-factor authentication for administrative access, air-gapped storage of root CA keys, and regular security audits to detect vulnerabilities.

Compliance with industry standards and regulations is a key function of CPs and CPSs. Many organizations must align their certificate policies with global security frameworks such as the Baseline Requirements of the CA/Browser Forum, the General Data Protection Regulation (GDPR), the Federal Information Processing Standards (FIPS), and the Payment Card Industry Data Security Standard (PCI DSS). Ensuring compliance with these regulations helps maintain trust in PKI and protects sensitive information from cyber threats.

Transparency and accountability are fundamental to PKI trust, and CPs and CPSs contribute to this by requiring CAs to undergo regular audits and third-party assessments. Independent security audits verify that a CA is following its published CP and CPS, ensuring that it is operating securely and adhering to industry best practices. Publicly available CPs and CPSs also allow relying parties, such as web browsers and enterprises, to review the security policies of a CA before trusting its certificates.

The evolution of cybersecurity threats and cryptographic advancements requires that CPs and CPSs be regularly updated. As new attack vectors emerge, such as quantum computing threats to traditional cryptographic algorithms, PKI policies must adapt to address these risks. Organizations must periodically review and revise their certificate policies and practices to incorporate post-quantum cryptography, blockchain-based identity verification, and other emerging security technologies.

Effective certificate policies and practice statements are essential for maintaining the integrity, security, and reliability of digital certificates in PKI. By clearly defining the rules for certificate issuance, validation, and revocation, CPs and CPSs help establish a robust and trustworthy digital security framework. Organizations that implement and adhere to strong certificate policies can ensure secure online transactions, protect sensitive data, and maintain compliance with industry standards, ultimately reinforcing trust in digital communications.

Public Key Cryptographic Standards (PKCS)

Public Key Cryptographic Standards (PKCS) are a set of cryptographic specifications developed to standardize the implementation of public-key cryptography. These standards, originally created by RSA Laboratories in collaboration with various security experts, provide guidelines for secure key management, encryption, digital signatures, and certificate handling. PKCS standards play a crucial role in ensuring interoperability between different cryptographic systems and applications, making them essential for modern cybersecurity frameworks, including Public Key Infrastructure (PKI).

PKCS standards address various aspects of cryptographic security, defining how keys, certificates, and encrypted data should be formatted and managed. They provide widely accepted protocols that enable secure communication, authentication, and data protection. Without these standards, cryptographic implementations would lack consistency, making it difficult for different systems to work together securely. By following PKCS specifications, developers can ensure that cryptographic applications function reliably and maintain compatibility with industry best practices.

One of the most widely used PKCS standards is PKCS #1, which defines the RSA Cryptography Standard. This standard specifies the mathematical algorithms and encoding methods used in RSA encryption and digital signatures. It includes guidelines for key generation, padding schemes to enhance security, and secure encryption methods. RSA encryption is one of the most commonly used public-key cryptographic methods, and PKCS #1 ensures that RSA implementations follow a uniform standard. The standard also defines signature schemes such as RSA-PSS (Probabilistic Signature Scheme), which enhances the security of digital signatures by incorporating randomness to prevent attacks.

Another important PKCS standard is PKCS #5, which defines the Password-Based Cryptography Standard (PBKDF2). This standard is used to derive cryptographic keys from passwords using a hashing algorithm combined with a salt and multiple iterations. PBKDF2 is widely used in password storage and key derivation processes, making it more difficult for attackers to perform brute-force attacks. By increasing the number of iterations, PKCS #5 ensures that computing the derived key requires significant computational effort, improving security against password-cracking techniques.

For cryptographic key storage and exchange, PKCS #8 defines the Private Key Information Syntax Standard. This standard specifies how private keys should be securely stored and transferred, ensuring that they remain protected from unauthorized access. PKCS #8 supports different encryption algorithms to secure private keys, preventing attackers from extracting sensitive cryptographic material from key files. It is commonly used in applications that require secure key storage, including secure email, digital signatures, and TLS/SSL implementations.

When dealing with encrypted data, PKCS #7 defines the Cryptographic Message Syntax (CMS), which is used for secure data exchange. PKCS #7 allows for the encryption, signing, and authentication of messages, making it a key component in secure email communication, such as S/MIME (Secure/Multipurpose Internet Mail Extensions). It also supports digital signatures, allowing users to verify the authenticity and integrity of encrypted messages. Many PKI-based security applications rely on PKCS #7 to format signed and encrypted data for secure transmission.

Certificate management is another critical area covered by PKCS standards. PKCS #10 defines the Certificate Signing Request (CSR) format, which is used when requesting a digital certificate from a Certificate Authority (CA). A CSR contains an entity's public key along with identifying information, allowing the CA to verify and issue a corresponding certificate. The PKCS #10 format ensures that CSRs are structured consistently, enabling interoperability between different PKI systems and CA implementations.

To facilitate secure certificate storage, PKCS #12 defines the Personal Information Exchange (PFX) format, which is used to bundle a private key, public key, and digital certificate into a single encrypted file. This format is commonly used in secure authentication systems, where users need to import and export certificates between different platforms. PKCS #12 files are password-protected, ensuring that private keys remain secure even if the file is accessed by unauthorized users.

For applications requiring digital signatures, PKCS #11 defines the Cryptographic Token Interface Standard, which provides a standardized interface for interacting with hardware security modules (HSMs) and smart cards. PKCS #11 enables applications to securely generate, store, and use cryptographic keys within hardware-based security devices. This standard is widely used in government, finance, and enterprise security systems where strong authentication and key protection are required.

In addition to these widely adopted PKCS standards, various other specifications provide additional guidelines for cryptographic security. PKCS #3 defines the Diffie-Hellman Key Exchange Standard, which describes a secure method for two parties to establish a shared secret key over an insecure network. PKCS #15 specifies cryptographic token information formats, allowing different smart card implementations to interoperate.

The evolution of cryptographic security has led to the modernization of PKCS standards, with some specifications being integrated into newer frameworks such as the Cryptographic Message Syntax (CMS) and RSA-OAEP (Optimal Asymmetric Encryption Padding). Many PKCS standards have also been adopted by international organizations, including the Internet Engineering Task Force (IETF) and the National Institute of Standards and Technology (NIST), ensuring their continued relevance in global security standards.

As cybersecurity threats evolve, PKCS standards continue to be essential in maintaining the security of digital communications, authentication mechanisms, and encrypted data storage. Organizations implementing PKI and cryptographic security rely on these standards to ensure consistency, interoperability, and strong protection against cyberattacks. Whether securing online transactions, encrypting sensitive information, or validating digital identities, PKCS standards provide the foundation for modern cryptographic security solutions.

Secure Sockets Layer (SSL) and Transport Layer Security (TLS)

Secure Sockets Layer (SSL) and Transport Layer Security (TLS) are cryptographic protocols designed to secure communications over the internet by providing encryption, authentication, and data integrity. These protocols are widely used in web browsing, email, instant messaging, and other online services to protect sensitive information from eavesdropping, tampering, and man-in-the-middle attacks. While SSL was the original protocol, TLS is its modern successor, offering improved security, stronger encryption algorithms, and resistance against vulnerabilities found in SSL.

SSL was first developed by Netscape in the mid-1990s as a means to encrypt internet communications, particularly for securing HTTP traffic. SSL 2.0 was the first widely used version, but it contained significant security flaws, leading to the development of SSL 3.0. SSL 3.0 introduced improved encryption mechanisms and handshake processes but was eventually deprecated due to vulnerabilities such as the POODLE (Padding Oracle On Downgraded Legacy Encryption) attack, which exploited weaknesses in SSL's padding mechanisms.

TLS was introduced as the successor to SSL with the release of TLS 1.0 in 1999. It was based on SSL 3.0 but included enhancements to encryption, authentication, and key exchange mechanisms. TLS versions continued to evolve, with TLS 1.1 and TLS 1.2 bringing further improvements in security. TLS 1.3, the latest version as of recent years, significantly reduces handshake latency, removes outdated cryptographic algorithms, and strengthens overall security by enforcing forward secrecy.

The primary function of SSL/TLS is to establish a secure communication channel between a client (such as a web browser) and a server (such as a website). This is achieved through a process known as the TLS handshake, which involves several steps to negotiate encryption settings, verify identities, and exchange cryptographic keys. The handshake process includes the following key phases:

Client Hello – The client initiates a connection by sending a "hello" message to the server, listing supported TLS versions, encryption algorithms, and other security parameters.

Server Hello – The server responds with its own "hello" message, selecting the most secure options that both the client and server support. The server also provides its SSL/TLS certificate, which contains its public key and is issued by a trusted Certificate Authority (CA).

Certificate Verification – The client verifies the server's certificate by checking its authenticity against trusted CAs. If the certificate is invalid, expired, or revoked, the connection is terminated.

Key Exchange – Both parties generate and exchange cryptographic keys for encryption. In earlier TLS versions, key exchange often used RSA, but modern TLS 1.3 relies on Elliptic Curve Diffie-Hellman Ephemeral (ECDHE) to provide perfect forward secrecy.

Session Encryption – Once the key exchange is complete, both parties use the shared encryption key to encrypt all subsequent data transmissions.

Once the handshake is successfully completed, encrypted communication begins, ensuring that any data exchanged remains confidential and protected from interception or modification by unauthorized parties.

SSL/TLS supports a variety of encryption algorithms, known as cipher suites, which dictate how encryption, key exchange, and authentication are performed. A cipher suite typically includes:

A key exchange algorithm, such as RSA or ECDHE, to establish a shared encryption key.

A symmetric encryption algorithm, such as AES (Advanced Encryption Standard) or ChaCha20, to encrypt transmitted data.

A hashing algorithm, such as SHA-256, to ensure data integrity and prevent tampering.

TLS 1.3 simplifies cipher suites by eliminating outdated algorithms such as RSA key exchange and SHA-1 hashing, enforcing more secure options by default. This prevents attacks like BEAST (Browser Exploit Against SSL/TLS), which exploited weaknesses in earlier SSL and TLS implementations.

The adoption of SSL/TLS is critical for securing sensitive online transactions, such as online banking, e-commerce, and login authentication. Websites that implement TLS correctly display a padlock icon in web browsers, indicating that the connection is encrypted. Websites without TLS protection are marked as "Not Secure" by modern browsers, warning users that their data could be intercepted by attackers.

SSL/TLS certificates, issued by trusted Certificate Authorities, play a key role in verifying website authenticity. These certificates follow the X.509 standard and include information about the domain, organization, and certificate expiration date. Different types of SSL/TLS certificates exist, including:

Domain Validation (DV) Certificates – Basic certificates that verify domain ownership without additional identity checks.

Organization Validation (OV) Certificates – Certificates that verify the legitimacy of the organization requesting the certificate.

Extended Validation (EV) Certificates – High-assurance certificates that require rigorous identity verification, often used by financial institutions and large enterprises.

To maintain security, SSL/TLS implementations must include certificate revocation mechanisms, such as Certificate Revocation Lists (CRLs) and the Online Certificate Status Protocol (OCSP). These mechanisms help prevent the use of compromised or expired certificates, ensuring that secure connections remain trustworthy.

One of the key security principles enforced by modern TLS implementations is Perfect Forward Secrecy (PFS). This ensures that even if a long-term private key is compromised, past communications remain secure because session keys are generated uniquely for each session. TLS 1.3 enforces PFS by default, making it significantly more resilient against key compromise attacks.

Despite its importance, SSL/TLS can still be misconfigured, leading to security vulnerabilities. Common misconfigurations include:

Using outdated SSL/TLS versions (SSL 3.0, TLS 1.0, and TLS 1.1), which contain known security flaws.

Supporting weak cipher suites, such as those using RC4 or 3DES encryption.

Failing to renew expired certificates, causing security warnings in browsers.

Not implementing HTTP Strict Transport Security (HSTS), which ensures that all connections use HTTPS instead of falling back to insecure HTTP.

To mitigate risks, organizations must regularly audit their SSL/TLS configurations, ensuring that only strong encryption protocols and secure cipher suites are enabled. Security tools such as SSL/TLS scanners can help detect vulnerabilities and recommend best practices for secure deployment.

As cybersecurity threats continue to evolve, the future of SSL/TLS will likely include quantum-resistant encryption algorithms, ensuring that encrypted communications remain secure against quantum computing attacks. Research into Post-Quantum Cryptography (PQC) aims to develop cryptographic methods that can withstand future computational advancements.

SSL and TLS have revolutionized internet security by enabling encrypted communications and establishing trust between clients and servers. While SSL has been deprecated due to security flaws, TLS continues to evolve, providing stronger encryption, faster performance, and improved resilience against attacks. Organizations and individuals must stay up to date with the latest TLS best practices to protect sensitive data, maintain privacy, and ensure secure online interactions.

Implementing PKI in Web Security

Public Key Infrastructure (PKI) plays a fundamental role in securing web applications, online transactions, and internet communications. It provides a structured framework for encryption, authentication, and data integrity, ensuring that users can trust the websites and services they interact with. Without PKI, sensitive data transmitted over the internet would be vulnerable to eavesdropping, identity spoofing, and various cyberattacks. Implementing PKI in web security involves deploying digital certificates, managing cryptographic keys, and ensuring secure communication through SSL/TLS protocols.

One of the most common applications of PKI in web security is securing websites through SSL/TLS certificates. These certificates, issued by trusted Certificate Authorities (CAs), enable encrypted communication between a client (such as a web browser) and a server (such as a website). When a user visits a website that uses HTTPS, their browser checks the website's SSL/TLS certificate to verify its authenticity. If the certificate is valid and trusted, the browser establishes a secure encrypted connection, protecting data from interception and tampering.

The process of implementing PKI in web security begins with obtaining and installing an SSL/TLS certificate. Website owners generate a Certificate Signing Request (CSR), which contains their domain name, public key, and organization details. This CSR is submitted to a CA, which verifies the requestor's identity before issuing a signed certificate. The issued certificate is then installed on the web server, allowing it to encrypt data transmitted between users and the website.

There are different types of SSL/TLS certificates based on the level of validation performed by the CA:

Domain Validation (DV) Certificates: These certificates only verify domain ownership and are commonly used for personal websites and blogs.

Organization Validation (OV) Certificates: These provide additional validation by verifying the organization's identity and legal status.

Extended Validation (EV) Certificates: These require strict identity verification and display the organization's name in the browser's address bar, enhancing user trust.

PKI also supports multi-domain and wildcard certificates, which allow website owners to secure multiple subdomains or domains under a single certificate. This simplifies certificate management and reduces costs for organizations that operate multiple websites.

Beyond securing website connections, PKI is used to authenticate users and devices accessing web applications. Client authentication certificates replace traditional username-password authentication by requiring users to present a valid digital certificate before accessing a system. This method enhances security by preventing unauthorized access, phishing attacks, and credential theft. Client authentication certificates are commonly used in enterprise networks, VPNs, and secure email systems.

PKI also plays a critical role in code signing, ensuring that software and web applications are not tampered with before reaching users. Code signing certificates, issued by CAs, allow developers to digitally sign their applications, proving that the software originates from a legitimate source and has not been modified by a third party. Web browsers and operating systems check these signatures before executing software, preventing malware from being installed on users' devices.

Another important aspect of PKI in web security is email encryption and authentication. Secure/Multipurpose Internet Mail Extensions (S/MIME) uses digital certificates to encrypt and digitally sign emails, ensuring that messages remain confidential and that recipients can verify the sender's identity. Email providers and enterprise email systems implement PKI-based solutions to prevent phishing attacks, email spoofing, and data breaches.

Managing PKI in web security requires proper certificate lifecycle management. Organizations must track certificate expiration dates, renew certificates before they expire, and revoke compromised certificates to prevent misuse. The failure to manage SSL/TLS certificates properly can lead to security warnings in browsers, service disruptions, and potential cyberattacks. Automated Certificate Management Systems (CMS) help organizations streamline the issuance, renewal, and revocation of certificates, reducing human error and administrative overhead.

Certificate revocation mechanisms, such as Certificate Revocation Lists (CRLs) and the Online Certificate Status Protocol (OCSP), are essential for maintaining trust in PKI-based security. CRLs provide a list of revoked certificates, while OCSP allows real-time status verification. Web browsers and security applications use these mechanisms to check whether a certificate is still valid before trusting it for secure communication.

For large-scale deployments, organizations implement Enterprise PKI (EPKI) solutions, which provide internal certificate issuance and management capabilities. EPKI allows businesses to create their own private CA for securing internal systems, employee authentication, and device management. This approach provides greater control over certificate policies and reduces dependency on external CAs for internal security needs.

As cyber threats evolve, PKI continues to adapt to new security challenges. The rise of quantum computing poses a potential risk to traditional cryptographic algorithms, prompting research into post-quantum cryptography (PQC). Organizations implementing PKI in web security must stay informed about emerging cryptographic standards to ensure long-term security. Additionally, advancements in blockchain-based PKI offer decentralized alternatives to traditional CA-based trust models, improving transparency and resilience against CA compromises.

PKI is a fundamental component of web security, enabling encrypted communication, user authentication, and data integrity. Proper implementation and management of PKI ensure that online services remain secure, protecting users from cyber threats while maintaining trust in digital interactions. Organizations that leverage PKI effectively can enhance their security posture, reduce risks, and comply with regulatory requirements for data protection and privacy.

Secure Email with S/MIME and PKI

Email is one of the most widely used communication methods in both personal and professional settings. However, standard email protocols do not provide built-in security, making messages susceptible to interception, tampering, and spoofing. Cybercriminals often exploit email vulnerabilities to conduct phishing attacks, impersonate legitimate senders, and distribute malware. To mitigate these risks, organizations and individuals implement Secure/Multipurpose Internet Mail Extensions (S/MIME), a PKI-based email security standard that enables encryption and digital signatures.

S/MIME is designed to enhance email security by providing message confidentiality, integrity, and authentication. It achieves this by using cryptographic techniques, specifically public key encryption and digital signatures, to protect email content and verify sender identities. As part of Public Key Infrastructure (PKI), S/MIME relies on digital certificates issued by trusted Certificate Authorities (CAs) to ensure that messages remain secure and verifiable.

The primary function of S/MIME is email encryption, which protects the content of an email from being read by unauthorized parties. When a sender composes an email and encrypts it using S/MIME, the recipient's public key is used to encrypt the message. Only the recipient, who possesses the corresponding private key, can decrypt and read the email. This ensures that even if the message is intercepted during transmission, it remains unreadable to unauthorized entities. Email encryption is especially critical for industries that handle sensitive information, such as financial services, healthcare, and government agencies.

Another important feature of S/MIME is digital signatures, which verify the authenticity and integrity of an email. When a sender signs an email using S/MIME, their private key is used to generate a unique digital signature that is attached to the message. The recipient can then verify the signature using the sender's public key, ensuring that the email was not altered during transmission and that it genuinely came from the stated sender. This prevents email spoofing and phishing attacks, where attackers attempt to impersonate trusted senders to deceive recipients.

Implementing S/MIME requires the use of digital certificates, which serve as electronic credentials that authenticate users and encrypt communications. These certificates are issued by Certificate Authorities (CAs), which verify the identity of users before granting them a certificate. An S/MIME certificate typically contains the user's name, email address, public key, and the CA's digital signature. Users must install these certificates on their email clients to enable S/MIME encryption and signing capabilities.

The process of securing email with S/MIME and PKI involves several steps:

Certificate Enrollment – Users obtain an S/MIME certificate from a trusted CA. This may involve submitting a request and undergoing identity verification.

Certificate Installation – The issued certificate is installed on the user's email client, such as Microsoft Outlook, Apple Mail, or Mozilla Thunderbird.

Key Exchange – Before encrypting an email, the sender must have the recipient's public key. This is typically exchanged via a digitally signed email or retrieved from a corporate directory.

Email Encryption – When composing a confidential email, the sender selects the encryption option, which encrypts the message using the recipient's public key.

Digital Signing – If authentication is required, the sender applies a digital signature using their private key. This signature verifies the sender's identity and ensures the email has not been altered.

Decryption and Verification – Upon receiving the email, the recipient's email client uses their private key to decrypt the message and verify the sender's digital signature.

While S/MIME provides strong security benefits, managing digital certificates can be complex, especially in large organizations. Enterprises often implement Enterprise PKI (EPKI) solutions to automate certificate issuance, renewal, and revocation. These solutions integrate with Active Directory (AD) and Lightweight Directory Access Protocol (LDAP) to distribute certificates to employees seamlessly. Automated certificate management reduces administrative overhead and ensures that employees always have valid encryption keys for secure email communication.

S/MIME certificate lifecycle management is crucial for maintaining security. Certificates have an expiration date, and expired certificates can no longer be used for encryption or digital signatures. Organizations must track expiration dates and renew certificates in a timely manner to avoid disruptions. Additionally, if a private key is compromised or an employee leaves the organization, the associated certificate must be revoked to prevent unauthorized use. Certificate Revocation Lists (CRLs) and the Online Certificate Status Protocol (OCSP) are used to check the status of certificates and ensure that revoked certificates are not trusted.

Although S/MIME is a widely adopted standard for secure email, it is not without challenges. One of the main issues is key management, particularly in environments where users frequently change devices or email accounts. If a user loses access to their private key, they will be unable to decrypt previously received encrypted emails. To address this, organizations implement key escrow solutions, where a copy of the encryption keys is securely stored and can be recovered if needed.

Another limitation of S/MIME is compatibility. Not all email clients and webmail services support S/MIME encryption and digital signatures by default. While most enterprise email solutions, such as Microsoft Outlook and Apple Mail, support S/MIME natively, web-based email platforms like Gmail may require additional configurations or third-party plugins. This can create interoperability issues when communicating with recipients using different email providers.

Despite these challenges, S/MIME remains one of the most effective methods for securing email communications. It is widely used in regulated industries, where compliance with data protection laws and security standards is mandatory. Regulations such as the General Data Protection Regulation (GDPR), Health Insurance Portability and Accountability Act (HIPAA), and Federal Information Security

Management Act (FISMA) require organizations to implement encryption and authentication mechanisms to protect sensitive email communications.

As cyber threats continue to evolve, advancements in PKI and email security are expected to improve S/MIME implementation. Emerging technologies, such as post-quantum cryptography (PQC), aim to enhance encryption resilience against future quantum computing attacks. Additionally, decentralized identity solutions and blockchain-based PKI may offer alternative approaches to managing digital certificates and verifying email authenticity.

S/MIME and PKI provide a robust framework for securing email communications, offering encryption for confidentiality and digital signatures for authentication. By implementing S/MIME effectively, organizations can protect sensitive data, prevent phishing attacks, and ensure compliance with security regulations. Proper certificate management, automation, and interoperability planning are essential for maximizing the benefits of S/MIME while addressing its operational challenges.

Code Signing and Software Integrity

Code signing is a critical security mechanism used to verify the authenticity and integrity of software, applications, and scripts. It ensures that software has not been tampered with and originates from a trusted source. Code signing is widely used in operating systems, software distribution, and mobile applications to prevent the execution of malicious or unauthorized code. By leveraging Public Key Infrastructure (PKI), code signing provides digital signatures that allow users and systems to verify the legitimacy of the software they install and execute.

The primary goal of code signing is to establish trust between software publishers and users. When software is signed, it includes a digital signature generated using the private key of the software publisher. This signature is attached to the executable file or script, allowing anyone who downloads the software to verify its origin. The verification process involves checking the digital signature against a trusted Certificate Authority (CA) to confirm that the code has not been altered since it was signed. If the signature is invalid, the software is flagged as untrusted, warning users against potential security risks.

Code signing certificates are issued by trusted CAs, which authenticate the identity of the software publisher before granting a certificate. These certificates come in different types, depending on the level of trust and validation required:

Standard Code Signing Certificates: These certificates verify the identity of the software publisher and ensure that the signed software is not modified after signing. They are commonly used for signing desktop applications, drivers, and scripts.

Extended Validation (EV) Code Signing Certificates: These provide a higher level of trust by requiring a rigorous verification process before issuance. EV code signing certificates offer additional security benefits, such as Windows SmartScreen reputation, reducing warning messages when users install software.

The code signing process follows a structured workflow to ensure security and integrity. It involves the following steps:

Generating a Code Signing Certificate – A software developer or company requests a code signing certificate from a trusted CA. The CA verifies the organization's identity before issuing the certificate.

Creating a Digital Signature – The software publisher generates a cryptographic hash of the software and encrypts it using their private key. This hash is unique to the software and serves as a fingerprint that verifies its integrity.

Embedding the Digital Signature – The signed hash, along with the certificate, is attached to the software file. This signature ensures that any modifications to the file will invalidate the signature, alerting users to potential tampering.

Verification by End Users – When users download and install the software, their system verifies the digital signature using the publisher's public key. If the signature is valid and the certificate is trusted, the software is allowed to execute.

One of the key security benefits of code signing is protection against tampering and malware injection. Without code signing, attackers could modify software to include malware, distribute altered versions, and trick users into installing malicious programs. Code signing prevents such attacks by ensuring that any changes to the signed code break the digital signature, alerting users that the software may have been compromised.

Another advantage of code signing is improved security for software distribution. Many operating systems, including Windows, macOS, and Linux, enforce strict security policies that require signed software before execution. Windows, for example, uses Windows Defender SmartScreen to block unsigned applications or display warnings to users. Apple's Gatekeeper system similarly prevents the execution of unsigned applications on macOS. These security features reduce the risk of running unverified or malicious software.

In addition to traditional software applications, code signing is essential for mobile app security. Mobile operating systems such as iOS and Android require all applications to be digitally signed before they can be installed from official app stores. Apple's App Store and Google's Play Store enforce strict code signing policies to prevent unauthorized apps from being distributed. Developers must sign their apps using certificates issued by Apple or Google, ensuring that only verified software is installed on user devices.

Code signing also plays a crucial role in firmware and driver security. Hardware vendors sign firmware and device drivers to ensure that only trusted updates are installed on user systems. This prevents attackers from injecting malicious firmware into critical system components. Microsoft's Kernel Mode Code Signing (KMCS) requires all drivers to be signed before they can run on Windows, reducing the risk of driver-based malware attacks.

Despite its security benefits, code signing is not without challenges. One of the biggest risks is the theft or compromise of code signing certificates. If an attacker gains access to a developer's private key, they can sign malicious software with a legitimate certificate, making it appear trustworthy. This has happened in several high-profile cyberattacks, where attackers used stolen certificates to distribute malware. To mitigate this risk, organizations use Hardware Security Modules (HSMs) to store private keys securely, preventing unauthorized access.

Another challenge is certificate expiration and revocation. Code signing certificates have a limited validity period, usually between one and three years. When a certificate expires, software signed with that certificate may no longer be trusted. To address this issue, developers use timestamping, which allows software to remain valid even after the signing certificate expires. Timestamping records the date and time the code was signed, enabling systems to verify that the software was signed with a valid certificate at the time of signing.

Certificate revocation is necessary when a code signing certificate is compromised or misused. CAs maintain Certificate Revocation Lists (CRLs) and use the Online Certificate Status Protocol (OCSP) to check whether a certificate has been revoked. If a revoked certificate is used to sign software, security systems can detect it and prevent execution, protecting users from potential threats.

To enhance security, best practices for code signing include:

Using strong cryptographic algorithms, such as SHA-256 and RSA-4096, to ensure the security of digital signatures.

Storing private keys in HSMs to prevent unauthorized access and key theft.

Implementing multi-factor authentication for code signing operations to add an extra layer of security.

Regularly rotating code signing certificates to reduce the impact of potential compromises.

Enforcing strict access controls on signing infrastructure to prevent insider threats.

As cyber threats continue to evolve, code signing remains a critical defense mechanism for software security. Future advancements in post-quantum cryptography (PQC) may introduce new signing algorithms to withstand quantum-based attacks. Additionally, blockchain technology is being explored for decentralized code signing, providing enhanced transparency and security.

Code signing and software integrity are fundamental to establishing trust in digital applications. By ensuring that software is authentic, untampered, and securely distributed, code signing protects users from malicious attacks, unauthorized modifications, and identity spoofing. Organizations that implement robust code signing practices can safeguard their software ecosystem, maintain user trust, and enhance the overall security of the digital landscape.

PKI in Virtual Private Networks (VPNs)

Virtual Private Networks (VPNs) play a crucial role in securing remote access to private networks, encrypting data transmissions, and ensuring the confidentiality of internet communications. They are widely used by organizations, businesses, and individual users to protect sensitive information from unauthorized access. Public Key Infrastructure (PKI) enhances the security of VPNs by providing a framework for authentication, encryption, and key management. By integrating PKI with VPNs, organizations can ensure that only authorized users and devices can establish secure connections, preventing cyber threats such as man-in-the-middle attacks, credential theft, and unauthorized access.

VPNs function by creating a secure tunnel between a user's device and a private network, allowing encrypted communication over the internet. This prevents third parties, such as hackers or internet service providers (ISPs), from intercepting or modifying transmitted data. There are various types of VPNs, including Remote Access VPNs, which enable employees to connect to a corporate network from remote locations, and Site-to-Site VPNs, which securely link multiple branch offices over the internet. Regardless of the VPN type, strong authentication and encryption mechanisms are essential to prevent unauthorized access and data breaches.

Traditionally, VPNs rely on username-password authentication to verify users. However, this method is vulnerable to attacks such as phishing, brute-force attempts, and credential leaks. To strengthen authentication, PKI introduces digital certificates, which serve as electronic credentials for users, devices, and VPN gateways. These certificates, issued by a trusted Certificate Authority (CA), replace or complement password-based authentication by verifying identities through cryptographic mechanisms.

The process of implementing PKI in VPN authentication involves several key components:

Certificate Issuance – The organization's CA issues digital certificates to users, devices, and VPN servers. These certificates contain a public key, a unique identifier, and the CA's digital signature.

Key Pair Generation – Each entity requesting a certificate generates a public-private key pair. The private key is securely stored on the user's device, while the public key is included in the certificate.

Certificate Distribution – The issued certificates are distributed to authorized users and VPN servers. VPN clients store their certificates in local keystores, ensuring they are available for authentication.

Mutual Authentication – When a VPN client initiates a connection, it presents its certificate to the VPN server. The server verifies the certificate against the CA's trusted certificate chain. The server also presents its own certificate to the client, establishing mutual trust before encrypting the session.

Secure Key Exchange – After authentication, the VPN client and server exchange encryption keys using protocols such as Diffie-Hellman (DH) or Elliptic Curve Diffie-Hellman (ECDH), enabling secure data transmission.

PKI enhances VPN security by eliminating password vulnerabilities and providing multi-factor authentication (MFA) options. Instead of relying solely on passwords, VPN implementations can enforce certificate-based authentication combined with smart cards, USB tokens, or biometric verification. This prevents unauthorized access even if passwords are compromised, significantly improving security posture.

Encryption is another critical aspect of PKI-enabled VPNs. VPN protocols such as IPsec (Internet Protocol Security) and SSL/TLS (Secure Sockets Layer/Transport Layer Security) rely on PKI for secure encryption key management. IPsec VPNs, commonly used in enterprise environments, encrypt IP traffic at the network layer using cryptographic keys derived from PKI certificates. SSL/TLS VPNs, used for web-based remote access, establish encrypted tunnels using digital certificates to authenticate servers and users.

One of the primary advantages of PKI in VPNs is scalability and centralized management. In large organizations, manually managing VPN credentials for thousands of employees is inefficient and prone to security risks. PKI simplifies credential management by allowing administrators to issue, renew, and revoke certificates through a centralized CA. When an employee leaves the organization, their VPN access can be immediately revoked by invalidating their certificate, preventing unauthorized connections.

PKI also enables role-based access control (RBAC) in VPN environments. By using certificate attributes and policies, organizations can enforce access restrictions based on user roles, departments, or security levels. For example, employees in the finance department may be granted access to internal financial systems, while IT administrators receive broader network privileges. This granular access control reduces the risk of unauthorized access and data breaches.

Despite its advantages, implementing PKI in VPNs requires proper certificate lifecycle management. Digital certificates have expiration dates, typically ranging from one to three years. If a certificate expires, the VPN client or server may lose access, disrupting operations. To prevent this, organizations use automated certificate renewal and monitoring tools to track expiration dates and issue replacements before disruptions occur.

Revocation is another critical aspect of PKI in VPNs. If a private key is compromised or an employee's access is no longer required, the corresponding certificate must be revoked immediately. This is done through Certificate Revocation Lists (CRLs) or the Online Certificate

Status Protocol (OCSP), allowing VPN servers to check whether a certificate is still valid before establishing a connection.

To enhance PKI security in VPNs, best practices include:

Using strong cryptographic algorithms such as RSA-4096 or ECC for key pairs to resist brute-force attacks.

Storing private keys securely using Hardware Security Modules (HSMs) or Trusted Platform Modules (TPMs) to prevent key theft.

Implementing certificate pinning, which ensures that only trusted certificates are accepted, preventing man-in-the-middle attacks.

Regularly auditing VPN access logs to detect suspicious activities and unauthorized connection attempts.

As cybersecurity threats evolve, the integration of PKI with VPNs remains essential for protecting sensitive network traffic. The rise of zero-trust security models further emphasizes the need for certificate-based authentication, where every device and user must be continuously verified before accessing network resources. Emerging technologies such as post-quantum cryptography (PQC) will also impact PKI-enabled VPNs, requiring organizations to adopt quantum-resistant encryption algorithms to future-proof their security.

PKI provides a robust and scalable solution for securing VPN access, offering strong authentication, encryption, and centralized certificate management. By replacing traditional password-based authentication with certificate-based security, organizations can significantly reduce the risk of unauthorized access, enhance data privacy, and ensure secure remote connections for employees, partners, and remote workers. Proper implementation of PKI in VPNs is a key component of modern cybersecurity strategies, ensuring secure and resilient network communications in an increasingly connected world.

Smart Cards and PKI Authentication

Smart cards play a vital role in Public Key Infrastructure (PKI) authentication by providing a secure and tamper-resistant method for storing cryptographic keys and digital certificates. These cards enhance authentication processes by ensuring that users, systems, and applications can verify identities using strong cryptographic techniques. Smart cards are widely used in corporate environments, government agencies, and financial institutions where secure access to systems and data is critical. By integrating smart cards with PKI, organizations can strengthen security, prevent unauthorized access, and eliminate reliance on weak password-based authentication.

A smart card is a small, portable device with an embedded microprocessor or memory chip capable of securely storing and processing cryptographic keys. Unlike traditional authentication methods that rely on passwords, smart cards leverage asymmetric cryptography to provide secure authentication. Each smart card contains a private key, which remains securely stored and is never exposed to the outside environment. The corresponding public key is included in a digital certificate, which can be verified by servers, applications, and authentication systems.

The authentication process using smart cards and PKI follows a structured workflow:

Certificate Issuance – A user is issued a digital certificate and a corresponding key pair. The private key is securely stored on the smart card, while the public key is included in the certificate issued by a trusted Certificate Authority (CA).

Smart Card Initialization – The smart card is configured with the user's certificate and cryptographic credentials, ensuring that only authorized users can access it. Some smart cards require a Personal Identification Number (PIN) for additional security.

Authentication Request – When the user attempts to access a system, they insert the smart card into a card reader or use a contactless interface. The authentication system requests proof of identity.

Challenge-Response Authentication – The system sends a challenge to the smart card, which signs the challenge using the private key stored on the card. The signed response is sent back to the system.

Verification – The system verifies the response using the public key in the user's certificate. If the verification succeeds, the user is granted access to the system.

This two-factor authentication (2FA) process ensures that authentication is based on something the user has (the smart card) and something the user knows (the PIN). This combination significantly enhances security compared to password-only authentication, which is vulnerable to brute-force attacks, phishing, and credential theft.

Smart cards are commonly used in corporate identity and access management to secure login credentials, protect confidential data, and enable secure remote access. Many organizations require employees to use smart cards for logging into workstations, accessing VPNs, and digitally signing emails or documents. Windows and macOS operating systems support smart card authentication natively, allowing organizations to enforce strict access control policies.

In government and military applications, smart cards are an essential component of identity verification. Programs such as the Common Access Card (CAC) used by the U.S. Department of Defense and the Personal Identity Verification (PIV) card for federal employees rely on smart cards for secure authentication. These government-issued cards store digital certificates used for encrypted email communication, signing official documents, and gaining physical access to restricted areas.

Smart cards are also used in financial services for secure banking transactions, payment authentication, and ATM access. EMV (Europay, Mastercard, and Visa) smart cards, commonly known as chip cards, use PKI-based authentication to prevent credit card fraud and unauthorized transactions. These cards require PIN authentication for added security, reducing the risk of unauthorized card use.

An additional benefit of smart cards is their ability to facilitate digital signatures, ensuring document authenticity and non-repudiation.

When a user digitally signs a document using a smart card, the private key stored on the card generates a cryptographic signature unique to the document. The recipient can verify the signature using the signer's public key, ensuring the document has not been altered. This feature is particularly useful for legal contracts, electronic invoicing, and secure email communication.

Despite their advantages, implementing smart card authentication requires proper key management and security policies. Organizations must ensure that private keys remain secure, and access to smart cards is controlled. Lost or stolen smart cards pose a security risk, as unauthorized individuals could attempt to use them for authentication. To mitigate this, organizations implement revocation mechanisms, such as Certificate Revocation Lists (CRLs) and Online Certificate Status Protocol (OCSP), to immediately invalidate compromised credentials.

Another challenge is smart card lifecycle management, which includes issuance, renewal, and deactivation. Organizations must track smart card expiration dates and ensure that employees replace them before they become invalid. Automated certificate lifecycle management systems help streamline this process by notifying users of upcoming expirations and simplifying renewal procedures.

Smart card adoption also depends on hardware compatibility and user convenience. While USB and NFC-enabled smart cards have improved accessibility, organizations must ensure that employees have the necessary readers or compatible devices. Some users may find smart card authentication cumbersome compared to biometric or token-based authentication methods. However, advancements in virtual smart cards aim to address this by emulating physical smart cards in secure environments, allowing users to authenticate without needing a physical device.

As security threats continue to evolve, multi-factor authentication (MFA) strategies increasingly incorporate smart cards alongside biometric authentication, mobile-based authentication, and security tokens. The integration of smart cards with biometric verification, such as fingerprint scanning, further strengthens authentication by ensuring that only the card's rightful owner can use it.

Looking ahead, post-quantum cryptography (PQC) will play a role in shaping the future of smart card security. Quantum computers pose a potential threat to traditional cryptographic algorithms, prompting research into quantum-resistant authentication methods. Smart cards must eventually support quantum-safe cryptographic protocols to maintain their role in high-security authentication.

Organizations implementing smart card authentication must follow best practices, including:

Enforcing strong PIN policies to prevent unauthorized card use.

Storing private keys securely within tamper-resistant smart card hardware.

Regularly updating and revoking certificates associated with lost or stolen smart cards.

Implementing multi-factor authentication by combining smart cards with biometrics or one-time passwords (OTPs).

Training employees on smart card security best practices to prevent misuse and unauthorized sharing.

Smart cards and PKI authentication provide a robust security solution for access control, digital signatures, and encrypted communication. By leveraging strong cryptographic authentication, organizations can protect sensitive data, prevent unauthorized access, and enhance overall cybersecurity resilience. As technology evolves, smart cards will continue to be a key element of identity verification and secure authentication in enterprise, government, and financial applications.

Two-Factor Authentication (2FA) and PKI

Two-Factor Authentication (2FA) is a security mechanism that enhances authentication by requiring users to provide two distinct forms of verification before gaining access to a system, application, or online account. Traditional authentication methods rely solely on passwords, which are vulnerable to brute-force attacks, phishing, credential stuffing, and data breaches. By adding a second layer of authentication, 2FA significantly reduces the risk of unauthorized access and identity theft.

Public Key Infrastructure (PKI) plays a crucial role in implementing strong 2FA solutions. PKI provides digital certificates, cryptographic keys, and secure authentication mechanisms that verify user identities beyond passwords. By leveraging PKI-based authentication, organizations can enhance security, ensure data integrity, and reduce reliance on easily compromised credentials.

2FA is based on the principle of requiring authentication from two of the following three categories:

Something You Know – A password, PIN, or security question answer.

Something You Have – A smart card, security token, mobile device, or digital certificate.

Something You Are – Biometric authentication such as a fingerprint, facial recognition, or retina scan.

A PKI-enhanced 2FA implementation typically involves a combination of digital certificates and physical or software-based authentication factors. This ensures that even if a user's password is stolen, an attacker cannot access the system without the additional authentication factor.

How PKI Enhances 2FA Security

PKI strengthens 2FA by providing cryptographic authentication, ensuring that only legitimate users can access protected resources. It enables the use of:

Digital Certificates for Identity Verification – Certificates issued by a trusted Certificate Authority (CA) serve as digital identities that authenticate users and devices. When a user logs in, the system verifies the certificate before granting access.

Smart Cards and Security Tokens – These physical devices store cryptographic keys and certificates, ensuring that authentication requires possession of the device in addition to a password or PIN.

Biometric Authentication and PKI – Some 2FA solutions integrate biometric authentication with PKI, ensuring that only authorized users can activate their digital certificates.

PKI-Based 2FA Authentication Methods

Smart Card-Based Authentication

Smart cards store digital certificates and private keys, allowing users to authenticate securely. When logging in, the user inserts the smart card into a reader and enters a PIN. The system verifies the certificate stored on the smart card before granting access. This method is widely used in government agencies, enterprises, and financial institutions.

USB Security Tokens

USB tokens function similarly to smart cards but connect directly to a computer via USB. They store cryptographic credentials and require users to enter a PIN or use biometric verification to authenticate. YubiKey and Feitian tokens are popular examples of USB-based authentication devices used for PKI-backed 2FA.

Software Certificates and Mobile Authentication

Users can store PKI certificates on mobile devices and use authentication applications to verify their identity. Mobile-based 2FA solutions, such as Google Authenticator or Microsoft Authenticator, generate time-based one-time passwords (TOTP) or push notifications that require user approval. Some implementations use PKI to validate the authenticity of mobile authentication requests.

Email and SMS-Based 2FA

Although not as secure as PKI-based authentication, some organizations use SMS or email-based 2FA, where a one-time password (OTP) is sent to the user's registered device. PKI can improve this method by encrypting messages or ensuring that authentication messages originate from a trusted source.

FIDO2 and WebAuthn with PKI

The FIDO2 authentication standard, supported by major browsers and platforms, enables passwordless authentication using PKI-backed security keys, biometrics, and hardware tokens. FIDO2-based authentication eliminates phishing risks and enhances 2FA security by leveraging public-key cryptography.

Benefits of Using PKI in 2FA

Stronger Security – PKI-based 2FA eliminates the risks associated with weak or reused passwords by introducing cryptographic authentication mechanisms.

Protection Against Phishing – Unlike traditional password-based authentication, PKI-backed 2FA methods prevent attackers from stealing credentials through phishing attacks.

Scalability and Centralized Management – Organizations can manage digital certificates, access policies, and authentication tokens centrally using Enterprise PKI (EPKI) solutions.

Regulatory Compliance – Many industries require strong authentication mechanisms to comply with regulations such as GDPR, HIPAA, and PCI DSS. PKI-based 2FA ensures compliance by enforcing strict identity verification and encryption standards.

Challenges of PKI in 2FA

Despite its security benefits, implementing PKI-based 2FA comes with challenges:

Key Management Complexity – Organizations must securely issue, store, and revoke digital certificates to prevent unauthorized access.

Hardware Costs – Smart cards, USB tokens, and HSMs (Hardware Security Modules) may require additional investment for large-scale deployments.

User Experience and Adoption – Some users may find PKI-based authentication more complex than traditional password-based methods, requiring training and support.

Future Trends in PKI and 2FA

As cybersecurity threats evolve, PKI-based 2FA will continue to be a cornerstone of secure authentication strategies. Emerging trends include:

Post-Quantum Cryptography (PQC) – As quantum computing advances, organizations will transition to quantum-resistant PKI algorithms to protect cryptographic authentication mechanisms.

Decentralized Identity Solutions – Blockchain and decentralized PKI models may enhance authentication by eliminating reliance on centralized certificate authorities.

Biometric-PKI Integration – Future authentication systems will combine PKI certificates with advanced biometrics for enhanced identity verification.

PKI provides a robust foundation for 2FA, ensuring that authentication is secure, scalable, and resistant to modern cyber threats. By integrating PKI with smart cards, USB tokens, mobile authentication, and biometric verification, organizations can implement a strong and resilient authentication framework that protects user identities and sensitive data.

PKI and Identity Management Systems

Public Key Infrastructure (PKI) plays a fundamental role in modern identity management systems (IDMS) by providing a secure and scalable framework for authentication, authorization, and digital identity verification. As organizations increasingly move toward digital transformation, managing identities securely across networks, cloud environments, and enterprise applications has become a critical challenge. PKI addresses these challenges by ensuring that digital identities are verifiable, encrypted, and protected against unauthorized access.

Identity management systems are designed to handle user identities, roles, permissions, and access rights within an organization. These systems ensure that only authorized users can access specific resources while preventing identity fraud and unauthorized access. By integrating PKI into identity management, organizations can enhance their security posture by replacing weak password-based authentication with strong cryptographic mechanisms, reducing the risk of credential theft and identity spoofing.

How PKI Supports Identity Management

PKI enhances identity management by providing:

Strong Authentication – Digital certificates replace or complement traditional username-password authentication, offering a higher level of security.

Identity Verification – Certificate Authorities (CAs) issue digital certificates that bind a user's identity to their cryptographic key pair, ensuring that authentication is based on verifiable credentials.

Access Control and Authorization – PKI enables organizations to enforce granular access control policies based on verified digital identities.

Secure Data Exchange – PKI encrypts identity-related data, ensuring that personal and sensitive information is protected against interception or tampering.

PKI integrates with identity management systems through digital certificates, which serve as electronic credentials that verify the authenticity of users, devices, and services. These certificates are issued by a trusted CA and contain the user's public key, identity details, and a digital signature to prevent forgery.

PKI in Enterprise Identity Management

Enterprises use PKI to strengthen identity management for employees, contractors, and business partners. This includes:

Enterprise Single Sign-On (SSO)

PKI integrates with SSO systems to enable seamless authentication across multiple enterprise applications. With a single digital certificate, users can access corporate systems without needing multiple usernames and passwords, reducing authentication fatigue and security risks associated with weak passwords.

Role-Based Access Control (RBAC)

PKI enables role-based authentication, where access permissions are granted based on a user's identity and assigned role. Digital certificates can store role information, allowing identity management systems to enforce least privilege access policies, ensuring that users only access the resources necessary for their roles.

Multi-Factor Authentication (MFA)

Identity management systems leverage PKI to implement MFA, requiring users to authenticate using both a password (something they know) and a digital certificate stored on a smart card or hardware token (something they have). This strengthens identity verification and protects against unauthorized access.

Identity Federation and Cross-Domain Authentication

PKI enables identity federation, allowing users to authenticate across different organizations and domains using a single digital identity. This is critical for federated identity management (FIM) systems, where organizations establish trust relationships to allow secure authentication across multiple entities. Protocols such as SAML (Security Assertion Markup Language) and OAuth use PKI to sign and encrypt authentication tokens, ensuring secure cross-domain identity verification.

PKI in Government and National Identity Systems

Governments worldwide use PKI for digital identity programs to issue secure electronic identification cards (eIDs), passports, and national identity credentials. These systems rely on PKI for:

Citizen Authentication – eIDs contain a digital certificate linked to an individual's national identity, enabling secure authentication for online government services.

Digital Signatures – Citizens can use PKI-based digital signatures for legally binding electronic transactions, reducing reliance on physical documents.

Healthcare Identity Management – PKI secures patient records and enables healthcare providers to verify patient identities and sign electronic prescriptions.

PKI in Cloud Identity Management

As organizations migrate to cloud-based environments, Cloud Identity and Access Management (IAM) solutions integrate PKI for enhanced security. Cloud IAM solutions leverage PKI for:

Secure API Authentication – Digital certificates authenticate cloud-based APIs and services, preventing unauthorized access.

Cloud-Based Single Sign-On (SSO) – Users authenticate to cloud applications using certificates stored in cloud-based identity providers such as Azure AD, Google Workspace, or AWS IAM.

Zero-Trust Security – PKI enforces continuous identity verification in zero-trust architectures, ensuring that users, devices, and workloads are authenticated at every access request.

Identity Lifecycle Management with PKI

Managing digital identities requires identity lifecycle management, which includes:

Certificate Enrollment – Users apply for a digital certificate, which is issued by a CA after identity verification.

Certificate Renewal – Digital certificates have expiration dates and must be renewed periodically to maintain security.

Certificate Revocation – If a user's credentials are compromised or their role changes, their certificate is revoked using Certificate Revocation Lists (CRLs) or the Online Certificate Status Protocol (OCSP).

Certificate Expiration Management – Organizations use Automated Certificate Management Systems (ACMS) to track certificate expiration dates and prevent authentication failures due to expired credentials.

PKI and Decentralized Identity Systems

Emerging identity management models explore decentralized identity solutions, where users control their own digital identities without relying on a central authority. Decentralized Identifiers (DIDs) and Self-Sovereign Identity (SSI) frameworks leverage PKI for:

Blockchain-Based Identity Verification – PKI ensures that decentralized identities can be cryptographically verified without a central CA.

Identity Portability – Users can store digital certificates in blockchain-based wallets and use them across different services.

Reduced Identity Fraud – Decentralized PKI reduces identity theft by allowing users to prove their identity without exposing sensitive personal data.

Challenges of Implementing PKI in Identity Management

While PKI provides robust security, organizations face challenges in implementation, including:

Complex Key Management – Maintaining cryptographic key security requires dedicated infrastructure, such as Hardware Security Modules (HSMs).

Scalability Issues – Managing a large number of digital certificates requires automation and integration with existing IAM solutions.

User Adoption – Employees and users must be trained to use PKI-based authentication methods effectively.

Regulatory Compliance – Organizations must comply with global security standards such as GDPR, NIST, and ISO 27001 when implementing PKI for identity management.

Future of PKI in Identity Management

As cybersecurity threats evolve, PKI will continue to be a core component of identity management. Future trends include:

Quantum-Safe PKI – Organizations will transition to post-quantum cryptographic (PQC) algorithms to protect digital identities against quantum computing threats.

AI-Powered Identity Verification – Artificial intelligence will enhance PKI-based identity authentication by detecting anomalies and preventing identity fraud.

Biometric-PKI Integration – Combining biometrics with PKI authentication will further strengthen digital identity verification.

PKI remains essential for securing identity management systems, providing strong authentication, encryption, and identity verification. By integrating PKI with enterprise, cloud, and government identity management solutions, organizations can ensure robust security, prevent identity fraud, and enable trusted digital interactions.

PKI in Enterprise Security

Public Key Infrastructure (PKI) is a fundamental component of enterprise security, providing authentication, encryption, and digital signatures to protect sensitive data, verify identities, and secure communications. As cyber threats continue to evolve, organizations must implement robust security frameworks to protect their assets, networks, and users from unauthorized access, data breaches, and identity fraud. PKI plays a crucial role in securing enterprise environments by ensuring that only authorized users, devices, and applications can interact within corporate systems.

Enterprises rely on PKI to establish a trust hierarchy that ensures the authenticity of digital identities. This is achieved through digital certificates issued by a Certificate Authority (CA), which binds public keys to verified identities. By integrating PKI into enterprise security, organizations can enforce strong authentication mechanisms, encrypt sensitive information, and provide non-repudiation for critical business transactions.

Authentication and Identity Verification

One of the primary applications of PKI in enterprise security is strong authentication. Traditional password-based authentication is vulnerable to brute-force attacks, phishing, and credential theft. PKI eliminates these risks by using certificate-based authentication, ensuring that only legitimate users and devices can access corporate resources.

Employee Authentication – Organizations issue digital certificates to employees, which are used for logging into workstations, accessing enterprise applications, and connecting to corporate networks. These certificates replace passwords, providing a more secure authentication mechanism.

Multi-Factor Authentication (MFA) – PKI enhances two-factor authentication (2FA) by requiring users to authenticate using both a password and a certificate stored on a smart card, USB token, or mobile device. This ensures that even if a password is compromised, unauthorized access is prevented.

Device Authentication – PKI verifies the identity of corporate devices such as laptops, smartphones, and IoT devices before granting them access to enterprise networks. This prevents unauthorized devices from connecting to internal systems.

Securing Enterprise Networks

PKI plays a crucial role in network security, ensuring that communications between users, servers, and applications are encrypted and protected from interception. This is particularly important for:

Virtual Private Networks (VPNs) – PKI enables certificate-based VPN authentication, ensuring that only authorized users and devices can establish secure connections to corporate networks.

Wi-Fi Security – Enterprises use 802.1X authentication with PKI to prevent unauthorized access to wireless networks. Devices must present a valid digital certificate to connect to the network, eliminating the need for shared Wi-Fi passwords.

Zero Trust Security – PKI enforces zero trust principles, requiring continuous verification of user and device identities before granting access to corporate resources.

Encryption and Data Protection

Enterprises use PKI to encrypt sensitive data, ensuring that confidential information remains secure both in transit and at rest. Encryption protects corporate communications, financial transactions, and sensitive documents from being accessed by unauthorized parties.

Email Encryption – PKI enables Secure/Multipurpose Internet Mail Extensions (S/MIME) to encrypt and digitally sign emails, preventing email spoofing and unauthorized access.

File and Disk Encryption – Enterprises use PKI-based encryption to protect stored data on employee devices, ensuring that sensitive files remain unreadable without proper decryption keys.

Cloud Security – PKI enhances cloud security by encrypting data stored in cloud environments and securing API communications between cloud applications.

Digital Signatures and Document Integrity

Digital signatures provide non-repudiation and integrity for enterprise transactions, legal documents, and contracts. By using PKI-based digital signatures, organizations can ensure that electronic documents remain unaltered and legally binding.

Legal and Compliance Documents – Enterprises use digital signatures to sign contracts, invoices, and legal agreements, ensuring compliance with regulations such as eIDAS and the ESIGN Act.

Software Code Signing – PKI is used in code signing to verify the authenticity of enterprise software and prevent unauthorized modifications. This ensures that enterprise applications are not tampered with before deployment.

Workflow Automation – Digital signatures enable automated approval processes, reducing the need for physical paperwork and improving efficiency.

Enterprise Certificate Management

Managing digital certificates across an enterprise can be complex, requiring automated certificate lifecycle management to track certificate issuance, expiration, and renewal. Organizations use Enterprise PKI (EPKI) solutions to simplify certificate management and reduce the risk of expired or compromised certificates disrupting business operations.

Automated Certificate Issuance – Enterprises use Certificate Management Systems (CMS) to issue and distribute certificates to employees, devices, and applications without manual intervention.

Certificate Revocation and Renewal – Expired or compromised certificates are revoked using Certificate Revocation Lists (CRLs) or

Online Certificate Status Protocol (OCSP), ensuring that outdated credentials cannot be exploited.

PKI Integration with Identity Management – Enterprises integrate PKI with Active Directory Certificate Services (ADCS) or other Identity and Access Management (IAM) platforms to enforce security policies and access control.

Regulatory Compliance and Risk Management

Enterprises must comply with industry regulations and security standards that mandate strong authentication, encryption, and data protection. PKI helps organizations meet these compliance requirements by providing a structured security framework.

General Data Protection Regulation (GDPR) – PKI-based encryption protects personally identifiable information (PII) from unauthorized access.

Payment Card Industry Data Security Standard (PCI DSS) – PKI ensures secure authentication for financial transactions and payment processing systems.

Health Insurance Portability and Accountability Act (HIPAA) – PKI encrypts electronic health records (EHRs) and protects patient data in healthcare environments.

National Institute of Standards and Technology (NIST) Guidelines – Enterprises implement PKI to meet NIST 800-63 authentication standards for securing digital identities.

Challenges of PKI in Enterprise Security

Despite its benefits, implementing PKI in an enterprise environment presents challenges, including:

Complexity of Certificate Management – Enterprises managing thousands of digital certificates require automated solutions to track and renew certificates.

Integration with Legacy Systems – Some enterprise applications may not support modern PKI implementations, requiring additional configuration.

User Training and Adoption – Employees must be educated on using digital certificates, smart cards, and certificate-based authentication securely.

Key Management Risks – Protecting private keys is essential, requiring Hardware Security Modules (HSMs) to prevent key compromise.

Future Trends in Enterprise PKI Security

As cyber threats evolve, enterprises are adopting advanced PKI solutions to enhance security. Key trends include:

Post-Quantum Cryptography (PQC) – Enterprises are preparing for the transition to quantum-resistant PKI algorithms to prevent future quantum-based attacks.

Decentralized PKI – Blockchain-based identity verification is emerging as an alternative to centralized certificate authorities (CAs).

Cloud-Based PKI Solutions – Enterprises are leveraging PKI-as-a-Service (PKIaaS) to manage certificate issuance and revocation in cloud environments.

Zero Trust Architectures – PKI is being integrated into zero trust security models, ensuring that every user and device is authenticated before accessing enterprise systems.

PKI is a cornerstone of enterprise security, enabling strong authentication, encryption, and digital trust across corporate networks, applications, and cloud environments. By implementing PKI-based security frameworks, enterprises can protect sensitive data, prevent cyber threats, and ensure compliance with industry regulations.

Digital Signatures and Legal Validity

Digital signatures have become a critical component of modern electronic transactions, providing authentication, integrity, and non-repudiation for digital documents. As businesses and governments transition from paper-based to digital processes, ensuring the legal validity of electronically signed documents is essential. Digital signatures, backed by Public Key Infrastructure (PKI), offer a secure and legally recognized method for signing contracts, agreements, and official documents.

A digital signature is a cryptographic mechanism that verifies the authenticity of a document or message. Unlike traditional electronic signatures, which may only consist of a scanned handwritten signature or a typed name, digital signatures use asymmetric cryptography to ensure that the document has not been altered and that the signer's identity is verified. This makes them significantly more secure and legally enforceable in many jurisdictions.

How Digital Signatures Work

Digital signatures rely on PKI-based encryption to generate a unique and verifiable signature for a document. The process involves the following steps:

Key Generation – The signer generates a key pair: a private key, which is kept secret, and a public key, which is shared with others.

Signing the Document – The signer's private key is used to create a cryptographic hash of the document, which is then encrypted to form the digital signature.

Attaching the Signature – The digital signature is embedded in the document, along with a digital certificate issued by a trusted Certificate Authority (CA).

Verification – The recipient uses the signer's public key to decrypt the signature and compare the hash with the original document. If they match, the signature is valid.

This process ensures that the signed document:

Has not been altered – If any modifications are made to the document after signing, the verification process will fail.

Is legally tied to the signer – The signature is unique to the signer and cannot be forged without access to the private key.

Provides non-repudiation – The signer cannot deny having signed the document, as their private key was used in the process.

Legal Validity of Digital Signatures

For digital signatures to be legally recognized, they must comply with regulations and legal frameworks established by different countries and international organizations. Many jurisdictions have enacted laws to standardize digital signature use and ensure their enforceability in court.

Global Digital Signature Laws and Regulations

United States – ESIGN Act and UETA

The Electronic Signatures in Global and National Commerce (ESIGN) Act and the Uniform Electronic Transactions Act (UETA) recognize digital signatures as legally equivalent to handwritten signatures.

These laws establish that a digital signature is valid as long as all parties consent to electronic transactions and the signature process ensures authentication, integrity, and consent.

European Union – eIDAS Regulation

The Electronic Identification, Authentication, and Trust Services (eIDAS) regulation defines digital signatures as legally binding across all EU member states.

eIDAS distinguishes between three types of electronic signatures:

Simple Electronic Signatures (SES) – Basic electronic marks that may not provide strong identity verification.

Advanced Electronic Signatures (AES) – Secure signatures linked to the signer's identity and created using cryptographic keys.

Qualified Electronic Signatures (QES) – The highest level of security, requiring a qualified trust service provider (QTSP) to issue digital certificates.

A QES is legally equivalent to a handwritten signature under eIDAS.

Asia-Pacific Laws

Countries such as China, India, and Australia have implemented PKI-based digital signature laws similar to those in the U.S. and EU.

India's Information Technology Act (IT Act, 2000) establishes the legal framework for digital signatures, requiring the use of licensed Certifying Authorities.

Other International Frameworks

The United Nations Commission on International Trade Law (UNCITRAL) provides model laws for electronic signatures, influencing national regulations worldwide.

The ISO/IEC 14516 standard outlines security and cryptographic best practices for digital signatures.

Use Cases of Legally Valid Digital Signatures

Digital signatures are widely used across industries where legal validity and security are crucial. Common use cases include:

Business Contracts and Agreements – Enterprises use digital signatures to sign employment contracts, vendor agreements, and financial transactions, ensuring document authenticity and reducing paperwork.

Government and Public Services – Many governments require digital signatures for tax filings, legal documents, and identity verification processes.

Healthcare and Medical Records – Digital signatures protect patient records, electronic prescriptions, and insurance claims while ensuring compliance with HIPAA (Health Insurance Portability and Accountability Act).

Financial Services – Banks and financial institutions use digital signatures for loan applications, account openings, and electronic fund transfers while adhering to regulations such as PCI DSS (Payment Card Industry Data Security Standard).

Real Estate Transactions – Buyers and sellers sign property agreements digitally, streamlining real estate transactions and reducing delays.

Challenges in Legal Acceptance of Digital Signatures

Despite widespread adoption, legal challenges and technical limitations can affect the enforceability of digital signatures.

Cross-Border Recognition – Different countries have varying standards for digital signatures, making international transactions complex. Some jurisdictions do not recognize foreign-issued digital certificates.

Certificate Expiry and Revocation – Digital signatures rely on certificates issued by a CA. If a certificate expires or is revoked, verifying past signatures becomes difficult unless timestamping is used.

User Trust and Adoption – Some businesses and individuals still prefer handwritten signatures due to concerns about security, legality, and usability.

Security Risks – While digital signatures are highly secure, if a private key is compromised, the authenticity of signed documents may be questioned.

Ensuring Long-Term Validity of Digital Signatures

To address potential legal challenges, organizations implement additional security measures:

Timestamping – Ensures that a digital signature was created at a specific date and time, even if the signer's certificate later expires.

Long-Term Validation (LTV) Certificates – Store validation data within the signed document to allow future verification.

Hardware Security Modules (HSMs) – Protect private keys from unauthorized access, ensuring that digital signatures remain secure.

Audit Trails and Logs – Maintain records of the signing process to provide evidence in legal disputes.

The Future of Digital Signatures and Legal Frameworks

As digital transformation accelerates, legal frameworks for digital signatures continue to evolve. Future developments may include:

Blockchain-Based Digital Signatures – Distributed ledger technology (DLT) could enhance decentralized trust models, ensuring that digital signatures are immutable and verifiable without a central authority.

Post-Quantum Cryptography (PQC) – As quantum computing advances, digital signature algorithms will need to adapt to ensure security against quantum-based attacks.

AI-Enhanced Identity Verification – Artificial intelligence may be used alongside PKI to enhance biometric authentication and prevent fraudulent signature attempts.

Digital signatures provide a secure, legally recognized method for signing documents and verifying identity. By complying with international regulations and using PKI-backed encryption, organizations can ensure that digital transactions remain legally binding, tamper-proof, and secure. As technology advances, digital signatures will continue to replace traditional handwritten signatures, driving efficiency and trust in the digital world.

Internet of Things (IoT) Security with PKI

The rapid expansion of the Internet of Things (IoT) has revolutionized industries by connecting billions of devices, from smart home appliances and industrial sensors to medical devices and autonomous vehicles. However, this interconnectivity also introduces significant security challenges, as IoT devices often process sensitive data and interact with critical systems. Ensuring the security of IoT ecosystems requires robust authentication, encryption, and integrity verification mechanisms. Public Key Infrastructure (PKI) provides a scalable and reliable security framework for protecting IoT devices, enabling them to communicate securely and authenticate each other in a trusted manner.

IoT security is particularly challenging because many IoT devices operate in uncontrolled environments, have limited computational resources, and rely on wireless communications that are susceptible to attacks. Traditional security approaches, such as static passwords and pre-shared keys, are inadequate for large-scale IoT deployments. PKI offers a more secure alternative by providing digital certificates, cryptographic key management, and automated authentication for IoT devices.

PKI for IoT Device Authentication

One of the key security concerns in IoT environments is device authentication—ensuring that only legitimate and trusted devices can connect to a network or exchange data. PKI-based authentication involves assigning a digital certificate to each IoT device, allowing it to prove its identity using cryptographic signatures.

The authentication process in IoT environments typically follows these steps:

Certificate Issuance – A trusted Certificate Authority (CA) issues a unique digital certificate to each IoT device. This certificate contains the device's public key, identity attributes, and the CA's digital signature.

Key Pair Generation – Each device generates a public-private key pair, where the private key remains securely stored on the device, ensuring it cannot be extracted by attackers.

Mutual Authentication – When an IoT device attempts to connect to a network or communicate with another device, it presents its certificate. The receiving system verifies the certificate's authenticity using the CA's public key, ensuring the device is legitimate.

Secure Communication – Once authentication is successful, devices establish an encrypted communication channel using TLS (Transport Layer Security) or other secure protocols to prevent data interception.

By using PKI for device authentication, IoT networks can prevent unauthorized devices from connecting, mitigating risks such as spoofing, unauthorized access, and botnet attacks.

Securing IoT Communications with PKI-Based Encryption

IoT devices frequently transmit sensitive data, including personal information, industrial control signals, and financial transactions. Ensuring the confidentiality and integrity of this data requires strong encryption. PKI enables end-to-end encryption by managing encryption keys and ensuring secure key exchange.

TLS/SSL Encryption for IoT Devices – IoT devices can use TLS/SSL certificates to encrypt communications, ensuring that data transmitted between devices and cloud platforms cannot be intercepted by attackers.

MQTT and PKI Integration – Many IoT applications use the MQTT (Message Queuing Telemetry Transport) protocol for communication. PKI strengthens MQTT security by enabling certificate-based authentication and TLS encryption for data exchanges.

Data Integrity Verification – PKI ensures that data transmitted between IoT devices remains unchanged by using digital signatures, which verify that the received data has not been altered.

Certificate Lifecycle Management in IoT

Managing digital certificates across millions of IoT devices presents challenges, including certificate issuance, renewal, and revocation. Proper certificate lifecycle management ensures that devices remain secure throughout their operational lifespan.

Automated Certificate Issuance – Enterprises use Automated Certificate Management Environments (ACME) or IoT-specific PKI platforms to issue and install certificates on connected devices without manual intervention.

Certificate Renewal and Rotation – IoT devices with long lifespans require periodic certificate renewal to maintain security. Automatic renewal mechanisms ensure that devices continue to use valid certificates without service disruptions.

Revocation of Compromised Devices – If an IoT device is compromised, its certificate must be revoked to prevent further network access. Revocation is enforced through Certificate Revocation Lists (CRLs) or the Online Certificate Status Protocol (OCSP), allowing networks to check if a device's certificate is still valid before trusting it.

PKI for IoT Device Provisioning and Secure Boot

One of the major security concerns in IoT deployments is device provisioning—the process of securely onboarding new devices to a network. PKI simplifies secure provisioning by ensuring that only trusted devices receive network credentials.

Secure Boot Mechanisms – PKI-based secure boot ensures that an IoT device runs only authentic and untampered firmware. The boot process verifies the firmware's digital signature, preventing attackers from installing malicious firmware or backdoors.

Zero-Touch Provisioning (ZTP) – Large-scale IoT deployments use PKI to enable zero-touch provisioning, allowing new devices to authenticate and join the network automatically without manual configuration.

Challenges of Implementing PKI in IoT

Despite its advantages, implementing PKI in IoT environments presents several challenges:

Resource Constraints on IoT Devices – Many IoT devices have limited processing power, memory, and battery life, making traditional PKI operations, such as certificate verification and encryption, computationally intensive.

Scalability Issues – With billions of connected devices, managing a vast number of digital certificates requires highly scalable PKI infrastructure capable of handling large certificate issuance and renewal workloads.

Key Storage Security – Storing private keys securely on IoT devices is challenging. Attackers who gain access to a device's private key can impersonate it, compromising the entire network. Hardware security modules (HSMs), Trusted Platform Modules (TPMs), and secure enclaves provide stronger key protection.

IoT Supply Chain Attacks – Attackers can target the IoT manufacturing and distribution process, embedding malicious code in devices before they reach end users. PKI-based firmware signing helps detect unauthorized modifications.

Future Trends in PKI and IoT Security

As IoT adoption grows, PKI will continue to evolve to meet emerging security challenges. Future trends include:

Post-Quantum Cryptography (PQC) for IoT – Quantum computing threatens traditional encryption algorithms. Post-quantum PKI solutions will ensure that IoT security remains resilient against quantum attacks.

Blockchain-Based PKI for IoT – Some researchers are exploring blockchain-based PKI models to eliminate reliance on central Certificate Authorities (CAs), improving decentralized trust in IoT networks.

AI-Driven IoT Security – AI and machine learning are being integrated with PKI to detect anomalies in IoT authentication and predict security breaches before they occur.

IoT Identity Federation – Federated identity management models will allow cross-network authentication, ensuring that IoT devices can seamlessly authenticate across different ecosystems using PKI.

PKI is a foundational security component for IoT, enabling strong authentication, encrypted communication, and lifecycle management of connected devices. By integrating PKI with IoT security frameworks, organizations can mitigate cyber threats, prevent unauthorized access, and establish trust in an increasingly connected world.

Mobile Device Authentication using PKI

As mobile devices become central to business operations, online transactions, and personal communications, ensuring their security is critical. Traditional authentication methods such as usernames and passwords are vulnerable to attacks, including phishing, credential stuffing, and brute-force attacks. Public Key Infrastructure (PKI) provides a robust framework for mobile device authentication, enabling secure access to corporate networks, applications, and sensitive data. PKI enhances security by leveraging digital certificates, asymmetric encryption, and cryptographic key management, ensuring that only trusted mobile devices can authenticate to enterprise systems and cloud services.

The Importance of Mobile Device Authentication

Mobile devices, including smartphones, tablets, and wearables, are increasingly used for accessing corporate resources, performing financial transactions, and communicating sensitive information. However, they are also common targets for cybercriminals. Unauthorized access to mobile devices can lead to data breaches, identity theft, and corporate espionage. Implementing PKI-based authentication strengthens mobile security by ensuring that authentication is based on verifiable cryptographic credentials rather than easily compromised passwords.

Mobile device authentication ensures:

Device and User Identity Verification – Ensures that only authorized mobile devices and users can access networks and applications.

Protection Against Unauthorized Access – Prevents attackers from using stolen credentials to access sensitive information.

Secure Communication – Encrypts mobile device communications to protect data from interception and tampering.

Compliance with Security Standards – Helps organizations meet regulatory requirements such as GDPR, HIPAA, and PCI DSS by enforcing strong authentication.

How PKI Enables Mobile Authentication

PKI secures mobile authentication by using digital certificates issued by a trusted Certificate Authority (CA). These certificates replace traditional username-password authentication with a more secure and scalable identity verification mechanism. The process involves:

Certificate Issuance – A mobile device is issued a unique digital certificate containing its identity details and a public key, signed by a trusted CA.

Key Pair Generation – The mobile device generates a public-private key pair, with the private key securely stored within the device or a hardware security module.

Mutual Authentication – When a mobile device attempts to connect to a corporate network, application, or VPN, it presents its digital certificate for verification. The server authenticates the certificate before granting access.

Encrypted Communication – Once authentication is successful, TLS (Transport Layer Security) encryption ensures that all communications between the mobile device and the network remain secure.

PKI-based authentication prevents unauthorized access by ensuring that even if an attacker steals a username and password, they cannot authenticate without possessing the private key stored on the mobile device.

PKI Authentication Methods for Mobile Devices

PKI enables multiple authentication mechanisms for mobile devices, ensuring security across different use cases.

Certificate-Based Authentication for VPNs and Wi-Fi

Mobile devices use PKI-based certificates to authenticate to corporate VPNs and enterprise Wi-Fi networks.

Unlike password-based authentication, certificate-based VPN authentication ensures that only registered mobile devices can establish a secure connection.

802.1X Wi-Fi Authentication – Enterprise wireless networks use EAP-TLS (Extensible Authentication Protocol - TLS) for certificate-based authentication, preventing unauthorized devices from accessing corporate Wi-Fi.

Mobile Device Management (MDM) and PKI Integration

Enterprises use MDM solutions to enforce security policies on corporate mobile devices.

PKI ensures secure device enrollment, allowing only trusted devices to receive corporate configurations and access internal systems.

MDM platforms distribute digital certificates to managed mobile devices, enabling seamless authentication to enterprise applications.

Secure Mobile App Authentication

PKI enables mobile applications to authenticate users using client certificates, removing the need for passwords.

Secure OAuth 2.0 and SAML-based authentication use PKI to sign authentication tokens, ensuring the integrity of authentication requests.

Biometric Authentication with PKI

PKI integrates with biometric authentication (such as fingerprint, facial recognition, and retina scanning) to provide strong identity verification.

A mobile device can use biometrics to unlock a private key stored securely in a Trusted Platform Module (TPM) or Secure Enclave before signing an authentication request.

Email and Document Signing on Mobile Devices

PKI allows mobile users to digitally sign emails and documents, ensuring integrity, authenticity, and non-repudiation.

Mobile email clients supporting S/MIME (Secure/Multipurpose Internet Mail Extensions) use PKI certificates to encrypt and sign emails.

Certificate Lifecycle Management for Mobile Devices

Managing digital certificates across thousands of mobile devices requires efficient certificate lifecycle management. Organizations must ensure that certificates remain valid, secure, and updated.

Automated Certificate Issuance and Renewal – Enterprises use Mobile Device Management (MDM) and Enterprise PKI (EPKI) solutions to automatically enroll, issue, and renew certificates for managed mobile devices.

Certificate Revocation and Recovery – If a mobile device is lost or compromised, its certificate must be revoked immediately using Certificate Revocation Lists (CRLs) or Online Certificate Status Protocol (OCSP).

Secure Key Storage – Private keys stored on mobile devices must be protected using hardware security modules (HSMs), TPMs, or encrypted key vaults to prevent extraction by attackers.

Challenges in Implementing PKI for Mobile Authentication

While PKI offers strong security benefits, implementing it on mobile devices comes with challenges:

Device Compatibility and Integration

Different mobile operating systems (iOS, Android, Windows) have varying levels of PKI support and certificate management capabilities.

Enterprise PKI solutions must support multiple device types and authentication methods.

Key Management and Security

If a private key is compromised, it could be used for unauthorized access.

Organizations must implement secure key storage mechanisms such as TPMs, Secure Enclaves, or cloud-based key management services (KMS).

User Experience and Adoption

Some users find certificate-based authentication more complex than traditional passwords.

Organizations must ensure a seamless user experience by integrating PKI with biometric authentication and single sign-on (SSO) solutions.

Scalability for Large Enterprises

Managing certificates for thousands of mobile devices requires automated provisioning and revocation.

Cloud-based PKI (PKI-as-a-Service) offers scalability, reducing the burden of on-premises certificate management.

Future Trends in PKI and Mobile Authentication

As cyber threats evolve, PKI-based mobile authentication will continue to adapt with new security advancements:

Post-Quantum Cryptography (PQC) – As quantum computers threaten traditional encryption algorithms, quantum-resistant PKI will be essential for securing mobile authentication.

Decentralized PKI (dPKI) – Blockchain-based decentralized identity management could reduce reliance on centralized Certificate Authorities, improving trust and security.

AI-Enhanced Mobile Security – AI-driven threat detection can help identify anomalous authentication attempts and prevent mobile identity fraud.

Passwordless Authentication with PKI – The future of mobile security will emphasize passwordless authentication, replacing passwords with certificate-based and biometric authentication.

PKI provides a scalable, secure, and efficient solution for mobile device authentication, ensuring strong identity verification, encrypted communication, and compliance with security regulations. By integrating PKI with VPNs, Wi-Fi authentication, mobile applications, and biometrics, organizations can enhance mobile security and protect against cyber threats, unauthorized access, and data breaches.

PKI in Cloud Computing

Public Key Infrastructure (PKI) plays a critical role in securing cloud computing environments by providing authentication, encryption, and digital signatures to protect cloud-based services, applications, and data. As organizations increasingly adopt cloud computing for scalability and operational efficiency, ensuring security across distributed cloud environments has become a top priority. PKI enables trust, identity management, and secure communication in cloud infrastructures, ensuring that only authorized users, devices, and services can access sensitive resources.

The Need for PKI in Cloud Security

Cloud computing environments introduce unique security challenges due to their multi-tenant architecture, remote accessibility, and reliance on internet-based services. Traditional security models, which rely on perimeter-based defenses, are insufficient for securing cloud-based assets. PKI provides a robust security foundation by ensuring:

Strong Authentication – Verifies the identities of users, applications, and devices accessing cloud resources.

Secure Data Transmission – Encrypts data in transit and at rest to prevent interception and unauthorized access.

Digital Signatures and Integrity Verification – Ensures that data, code, and transactions in the cloud remain unaltered.

Scalability and Automation – Enables enterprises to issue, manage, and revoke certificates dynamically as cloud services scale.

PKI-Enabled Authentication in Cloud Computing

One of the key applications of PKI in cloud computing is authentication. Cloud service providers (CSPs) and enterprises use certificate-based authentication to verify identities and prevent unauthorized access. PKI-based authentication replaces weak password-based authentication with digital certificates, which are cryptographically bound to users, devices, and cloud services.

User Authentication – Cloud-based applications require multi-factor authentication (MFA) to ensure secure access. PKI enhances MFA by requiring a certificate-based authentication factor, ensuring that users authenticate using digital certificates stored on smart cards, USB tokens, or mobile devices.

Machine and Service Authentication – Cloud workloads, virtual machines, containers, and microservices require authentication to interact securely. PKI enables certificate-based service authentication, ensuring that cloud services communicate securely using trusted cryptographic credentials.

Zero-Trust Security Model – PKI aligns with zero-trust architectures by requiring continuous authentication and authorization of users and devices before granting access to cloud resources.

Encryption and Data Protection in Cloud Environments

Cloud computing requires strong encryption mechanisms to protect sensitive data from unauthorized access. PKI provides encryption key management and secure key distribution, ensuring that data remains protected in storage, transit, and processing.

TLS/SSL Encryption for Cloud Applications – Cloud-based services use TLS/SSL certificates issued by trusted Certificate Authorities (CAs) to encrypt web traffic and prevent man-in-the-middle attacks.

Cloud Storage Encryption – Enterprises implement end-to-end encryption using PKI-managed encryption keys to protect cloud-stored data from external and internal threats.

Hybrid and Multi-Cloud Security – Organizations using hybrid cloud or multi-cloud deployments rely on PKI to enable secure cross-cloud communication, ensuring that data shared between different cloud providers remains encrypted.

PKI in Cloud-Based Identity and Access Management (IAM)

Cloud providers offer Identity and Access Management (IAM) solutions to control access to cloud resources. PKI integrates with IAM frameworks to enhance identity security:

Federated Identity Management – PKI enables Single Sign-On (SSO) and federated authentication across multiple cloud applications using SAML (Security Assertion Markup Language), OAuth, and OpenID Connect.

Role-Based Access Control (RBAC) – Digital certificates can store identity attributes that define user roles and access permissions, ensuring that only authorized users can perform specific actions within the cloud.

API Security and Authentication – Cloud-native applications expose APIs (Application Programming Interfaces) that require secure authentication. PKI enables mutual TLS (mTLS) authentication for APIs, ensuring that only trusted clients can interact with cloud services.

Cloud PKI and Certificate Lifecycle Management

Managing digital certificates in cloud environments requires automation and scalability. Cloud PKI solutions streamline certificate issuance, renewal, and revocation to prevent service disruptions and security vulnerabilities.

Cloud-Based Certificate Authorities (Cloud CAs) – Many organizations use PKI-as-a-Service (PKIaaS) to issue and manage certificates without deploying on-premises infrastructure. Leading cloud providers, including AWS, Microsoft Azure, and Google Cloud, offer managed PKI services to simplify certificate management.

Automated Certificate Renewal – Cloud PKI integrates with ACME (Automated Certificate Management Environment) protocols to automatically renew expiring certificates, reducing manual intervention.

Certificate Revocation and OCSP – Cloud services use Online Certificate Status Protocol (OCSP) and Certificate Revocation Lists (CRLs) to revoke compromised or expired certificates dynamically.

Challenges of Implementing PKI in Cloud Computing

Despite its advantages, implementing PKI in cloud environments presents several challenges:

Key Management Complexity – Cloud environments generate a high volume of encryption keys and certificates, requiring robust Key Management Systems (KMS) to prevent unauthorized key access.

Scalability of PKI Infrastructure – Cloud-native applications require dynamic certificate provisioning for containers, microservices, and virtual machines. Enterprises must deploy scalable PKI solutions that support large-scale deployments.

Integration with Cloud Security Controls – PKI must integrate with cloud-native security solutions, including Identity and Access Management (IAM), Security Information and Event Management (SIEM), and Cloud Access Security Brokers (CASB).

Cloud Shared Responsibility Model – Cloud security operates under a shared responsibility model, where the cloud provider secures the infrastructure while the customer is responsible for securing data and identities. Organizations must implement PKI-based security policies to protect cloud assets.

Future Trends in Cloud PKI Security

As cloud adoption grows, PKI continues to evolve to address emerging security challenges:

Post-Quantum Cryptography (PQC) for Cloud Security – Quantum computing threatens traditional encryption algorithms. Cloud providers are investing in quantum-resistant PKI solutions to protect cloud communications from future quantum-based attacks.

Decentralized PKI (dPKI) for Cloud Identity Management – Blockchain-based decentralized identity systems are being explored to enhance trust in cloud authentication, eliminating reliance on centralized CAs.

AI-Driven PKI Automation – AI and machine learning are being integrated into cloud PKI solutions to detect anomalous authentication behavior, certificate misuse, and potential security breaches.

Zero-Trust Network Access (ZTNA) and Cloud PKI – As enterprises adopt zero-trust security models, PKI will play a critical role in continuous identity verification and policy-based access control for cloud applications.

PKI provides the foundation of trust in cloud computing, securing user authentication, data encryption, and cloud-native applications. By implementing PKI-as-a-Service, automated certificate management, and cloud-integrated identity solutions, organizations can enhance cloud security, protect sensitive data, and ensure compliance with evolving cybersecurity regulations.

PKI for Government and Military Applications

Public Key Infrastructure (PKI) is a foundational security technology used by governments and military organizations to protect sensitive data, enforce strong authentication, and ensure secure communication. Given the high-stakes nature of government and military operations, securing classified information, critical infrastructure, and digital identities is a top priority. PKI enables encryption, digital signatures, and certificate-based authentication, ensuring that only authorized personnel, devices, and systems can access restricted resources.

Governments and defense agencies operate in high-risk environments where cyber threats, espionage, and data breaches pose significant risks. PKI provides a scalable and robust framework for securing communications, digital transactions, and identity management in government and military sectors. By implementing PKI, these entities can prevent unauthorized access, cyberattacks, and data leaks while ensuring compliance with national security policies and global cybersecurity standards.

PKI for Secure Government Identity Management

Government agencies manage vast amounts of personally identifiable information (PII), including citizen records, tax filings, healthcare data, and legal documents. PKI strengthens identity verification and ensures that digital identities are securely issued, managed, and authenticated.

e-Government and Digital ID Programs – Many countries use PKI-based digital identity systems to issue electronic national ID cards (eIDs), passports, and driver's licenses. These digital identities allow citizens to securely access government services, sign legal documents, and authenticate online transactions.

Biometric and Multi-Factor Authentication (MFA) – Governments integrate PKI with biometric authentication, such as fingerprint and facial recognition, ensuring strong identity verification for accessing government systems.

Digital Signatures for Official Documents – PKI enables legally binding digital signatures for contracts, tax filings, and government-issued permits, ensuring document authenticity and reducing reliance on paper-based workflows.

Interagency Identity Federation – PKI supports federated identity management, allowing secure authentication across different government agencies without requiring multiple login credentials.

PKI in Military and Defense Security

Military organizations handle classified communications, mission-critical operations, and sensitive intelligence data. PKI plays a critical role in ensuring secure communications, device authentication, and encrypted transmissions across defense networks.

Classified Communication Encryption – PKI enables end-to-end encryption for military-grade messaging systems, secure email, and battlefield communications, preventing adversaries from intercepting sensitive information.

Military Personnel Authentication – Soldiers, officers, and defense contractors use smart cards embedded with PKI certificates to authenticate themselves when accessing military networks, weapons systems, and secured facilities.

Secure Battlefield Communications – Military forces use PKI-backed encryption in tactical radio systems, satellite communications, and drone command systems, ensuring secure data exchange in combat scenarios.

Military Internet of Things (IoT) Security – PKI is essential for securing autonomous defense systems, UAVs (unmanned aerial vehicles), and sensor networks, ensuring that only trusted military devices can communicate within classified networks.

PKI for Critical Infrastructure Protection

Governments are responsible for securing national critical infrastructure, including power grids, water supply, transportation systems, and emergency services. PKI enhances security by ensuring strong authentication and encryption for industrial control systems (ICS), supervisory control and data acquisition (SCADA) networks, and IoT-based infrastructure components.

Smart Grid Security – PKI authenticates smart meters and secures communications within the electrical grid, preventing cyber threats such as grid hacking, data manipulation, and sabotage.

Transport and Border Security – Governments implement PKI-based electronic passports (ePassports) and biometric access controls at border checkpoints, airports, and maritime security stations.

Disaster Response and Emergency Communications – PKI ensures secure communication channels between government agencies, emergency responders, and law enforcement during crises and natural disasters.

PKI in Secure Email and Classified Data Protection

Government agencies require secure email communication to protect classified information from cyber espionage and data leaks. S/MIME (Secure/Multipurpose Internet Mail Extensions), a PKI-based email encryption standard, ensures that government officials, diplomats, and military personnel can exchange secure, authenticated emails.

Email Encryption for Government Officials – PKI encrypts emails between government agencies, ensuring that classified communications remain confidential.

Digital Signatures for Email Authentication – Government personnel digitally sign emails to verify sender authenticity and prevent email spoofing.

Preventing Insider Threats – PKI enforces access control policies that restrict unauthorized employees from viewing or forwarding sensitive emails.

Military and Government PKI Certificate Management

Managing thousands to millions of digital certificates in government and military environments requires robust certificate lifecycle management to prevent security lapses.

Automated Certificate Issuance – Government PKI solutions use Automated Certificate Management (ACM) to issue, renew, and revoke certificates efficiently.

Certificate Revocation and OCSP – If a military officer's smart card is lost, or a government contractor's credentials are compromised, PKI enforces immediate certificate revocation through Certificate Revocation Lists (CRLs) and Online Certificate Status Protocol (OCSP).

Secure Key Management – Governments store PKI private keys in Hardware Security Modules (HSMs) to prevent unauthorized access and cryptographic key theft.

Challenges in Government and Military PKI Implementation

While PKI enhances security, implementing it in government and military sectors presents several challenges:

National Security Compliance and Regulations

Governments must comply with strict security policies, national cybersecurity laws, and intelligence-sharing agreements to prevent cyber threats.

Military PKI systems must adhere to NIST (National Institute of Standards and Technology), NATO security guidelines, and Federal Information Processing Standards (FIPS 140-2).

Large-Scale Certificate Management

Managing millions of digital identities across government agencies requires automated PKI infrastructure to handle authentication requests efficiently.

Integration with Legacy Systems

Many government IT infrastructures still rely on legacy systems that require PKI modernization to support cloud security, mobile authentication, and zero-trust architectures.

Cyber Warfare and Nation-State Threats

Governments must defend against nation-state cyberattacks that target classified databases, communication networks, and military command systems.

PKI helps protect against supply chain attacks, insider threats, and espionage tactics.

Future Trends in PKI for Government and Military Security

As cyber threats evolve, government and military PKI systems must adapt to emerging security technologies:

Post-Quantum Cryptography (PQC) – Military PKI systems are transitioning to quantum-resistant encryption algorithms to withstand future quantum computing attacks.

Blockchain-Based Identity Verification – Some governments are exploring blockchain-based PKI for decentralized identity management and tamper-proof digital certificates.

AI-Powered Cyber Defense – Artificial Intelligence (AI) and machine learning are being integrated into PKI monitoring systems to detect anomalous authentication behavior and insider threats.

Zero Trust Security Frameworks – PKI is becoming a core component of zero trust architectures, ensuring continuous authentication for government and military networks.

PKI is essential for securing government and military operations, providing strong identity authentication, encrypted communication, and cyber resilience against evolving threats. Governments and defense agencies must continuously modernize PKI infrastructure to adapt to emerging cybersecurity challenges, nation-state attacks, and future warfare technologies.

PKI in Financial Services and Banking

Public Key Infrastructure (PKI) is a fundamental security framework in the financial services and banking industry, ensuring the protection of sensitive financial transactions, customer identities, and digital banking services. As financial institutions increasingly transition to digital platforms, securing online banking, payment systems, and financial communications has become critical. PKI provides encryption, authentication, and digital signatures to safeguard transactions, prevent fraud, and ensure compliance with strict regulatory requirements.

The Role of PKI in Financial Security

Banks and financial institutions handle vast amounts of sensitive customer data, including account information, credit card details, and payment credentials. A breach of this information could lead to identity theft, financial fraud, and regulatory penalties. PKI addresses these security challenges by:

Authenticating customers, employees, and financial systems to prevent unauthorized access.

Encrypting financial transactions to protect sensitive data from cybercriminals.

Ensuring transaction integrity by using digital signatures that verify the authenticity of electronic payments and financial records.

Enhancing regulatory compliance with security standards such as PCI DSS, GDPR, PSD2, and Basel III.

PKI for Secure Online and Mobile Banking

As customers increasingly use online and mobile banking to manage their finances, securing these platforms is a top priority for financial institutions. PKI strengthens security by providing certificate-based authentication and encryption, ensuring that only authorized users can access their accounts.

Customer Authentication with Digital Certificates – Banks issue PKI-based digital certificates to customers for secure authentication when accessing online banking portals. This eliminates reliance on passwords, which are vulnerable to phishing and credential theft.

Multi-Factor Authentication (MFA) for Online Banking – PKI enhances MFA by requiring customers to authenticate using a combination of a password (something they know) and a digital certificate stored on a smart card or mobile device (something they have).

End-to-End Encryption for Banking Transactions – Online banking communications are encrypted using TLS/SSL certificates, ensuring that sensitive financial data remains protected during transmission.

PKI in Payment Systems and Digital Transactions

Financial transactions require integrity, confidentiality, and non-repudiation to prevent fraud and unauthorized modifications. PKI enables secure digital payments, credit card transactions, and mobile wallet authentication by ensuring that transaction data is encrypted, signed, and verified before being processed.

EMV Chip Card Authentication – PKI secures EMV (Europay, Mastercard, and Visa) chip card transactions, ensuring that only legitimate cardholders can make purchases. Chip cards use public key cryptography to authenticate transactions and prevent card cloning.

Secure Online Payments (3D Secure) – PKI is integrated into payment authentication protocols such as 3D Secure (Visa Secure, Mastercard SecureCode) to provide strong customer authentication (SCA) for online purchases.

Mobile Payment Security – Digital wallets and mobile payment platforms like Apple Pay, Google Pay, and Samsung Pay use PKI-based tokenization to secure transaction data and prevent unauthorized payments.

Digital Signatures for Financial Agreements and Contracts

Banks and financial institutions handle large volumes of legal agreements, loan applications, and electronic contracts. PKI enables digital signatures, ensuring that these documents are legally binding, tamper-proof, and verifiable.

Digital Signatures for Loan Applications – Customers and financial institutions can sign loan agreements, mortgages, and credit applications using PKI-backed electronic signatures, reducing paperwork and improving efficiency.

Regulatory Compliance with eIDAS and ESIGN – Financial institutions comply with eIDAS (Electronic Identification and Trust Services) in the EU and the ESIGN Act in the US, which mandate the use of digital signatures for legally binding electronic transactions.

Preventing Fraud in Financial Documents – Digital signatures ensure that contracts and financial reports remain unchanged, preventing fraudsters from altering sensitive financial data.

PKI in Financial Messaging and Secure Communications

Financial institutions exchange sensitive data daily through secure messaging systems, which require strong authentication and encryption to prevent cyber espionage, phishing attacks, and data breaches. PKI is used in financial messaging protocols, ensuring end-to-end security in banking communications.

SWIFT Network Security – The SWIFT (Society for Worldwide Interbank Financial Telecommunication) network, which facilitates international bank transactions, uses PKI-based encryption and authentication to secure interbank communications.

S/MIME for Secure Email Communication – Banks use S/MIME (Secure/Multipurpose Internet Mail Extensions) to encrypt and digitally sign emails, preventing phishing attacks and ensuring that sensitive financial emails remain secure.

Digital Certificates for Secure API Transactions – PKI secures Open Banking APIs, allowing third-party financial services to securely interact with banking systems without exposing customer credentials.

PKI for Fraud Prevention and Identity Verification

Fraud and identity theft remain major concerns in the financial industry. PKI helps prevent fraud by ensuring secure identity verification, transaction monitoring, and biometric authentication.

PKI-Enabled Biometric Authentication – Banks use biometric authentication (fingerprint, facial recognition, iris scanning) combined with PKI digital certificates to verify customer identities before authorizing transactions.

Tokenization for Secure Credit Card Transactions – PKI supports tokenization, replacing sensitive credit card data with cryptographic tokens that are useless if stolen.

Behavioral Analytics and PKI – Financial institutions integrate PKI with AI-driven fraud detection systems to monitor transaction patterns and identify suspicious activities.

Managing PKI Certificates in Financial Institutions

Managing digital certificates across a global financial network requires efficient PKI certificate lifecycle management to ensure that all transactions remain secure and compliant.

Automated Certificate Management – Banks use Automated Certificate Management Environments (ACME) to issue, renew, and revoke certificates for financial applications dynamically.

Certificate Revocation Lists (CRLs) and OCSP – Financial institutions monitor certificate revocation lists (CRLs) and use the Online Certificate Status Protocol (OCSP) to revoke compromised certificates instantly.

Hardware Security Modules (HSMs) for Key Storage – Banks store cryptographic keys in HSMs, preventing unauthorized access to sensitive financial data.

Challenges of Implementing PKI in Banking

Despite its security benefits, implementing PKI in financial services presents challenges:

Scalability and Performance – Financial institutions process millions of transactions per day, requiring PKI solutions that can scale efficiently.

Regulatory Compliance Complexity – Banks must comply with multiple regulations across different jurisdictions, making PKI governance complex.

Fraudulent Certificate Issuance – If a malicious actor obtains a fraudulent digital certificate, they could impersonate financial institutions and conduct unauthorized transactions.

Legacy System Integration – Some banks still operate on legacy IT infrastructures that require modernization to support PKI-based security.

Future Trends in PKI for Financial Services

As financial technology evolves, PKI will continue to play a crucial role in securing next-generation banking services.

Post-Quantum Cryptography (PQC) in Banking – Banks are preparing for quantum-safe encryption algorithms to protect financial transactions from future quantum-based threats.

Decentralized Identity (DID) in Financial Services – Blockchain-based decentralized PKI (dPKI) is being explored for self-sovereign digital identity management in banking.

AI-Powered Fraud Detection with PKI – AI-driven analytics will enhance PKI-based authentication by identifying anomalous transaction behaviors in real time.

PKI remains a critical security pillar in financial services and banking, ensuring secure digital transactions, fraud prevention, and compliance with regulatory standards. By integrating certificate-based authentication, encryption, and digital signatures, financial institutions can enhance security, protect customer identities, and build trust in the digital economy.

PKI in Healthcare and Electronic Health Records (EHR)

Public Key Infrastructure (PKI) is a vital component of security in the healthcare industry, ensuring the protection of electronic health records (EHRs), patient data, medical communications, and healthcare transactions. As healthcare systems become increasingly digital, protecting sensitive patient information from cyber threats, unauthorized access, and regulatory non-compliance is critical. PKI provides authentication, encryption, and digital signatures, enabling healthcare providers, patients, and third-party vendors to securely access and share medical data while ensuring integrity and privacy.

The Importance of Security in Healthcare

Healthcare organizations handle large volumes of personally identifiable information (PII) and protected health information (PHI), including medical histories, prescriptions, insurance details, and laboratory results. Cyberattacks targeting healthcare data have risen dramatically, with threats such as ransomware, phishing, and insider breaches putting patient safety at risk. PKI ensures that only authorized users and systems can access or modify patient records while securing digital communications within healthcare networks.

The implementation of PKI in healthcare supports:

Strong authentication – Ensuring that only authorized healthcare professionals, patients, and medical devices can access sensitive data.

Data encryption – Protecting patient information from unauthorized access and interception.

Regulatory compliance – Meeting legal requirements such as HIPAA (Health Insurance Portability and Accountability Act), GDPR, and HITECH (Health Information Technology for Economic and Clinical Health Act).

Medical device security – Authenticating and encrypting communications between Internet of Medical Things (IoMT) devices and healthcare networks.

PKI for Securing Electronic Health Records (EHRs)

Electronic Health Records (EHRs) have revolutionized patient care by allowing healthcare providers to store, access, and share medical records electronically. However, without strong security controls, EHR systems become targets for cybercriminals attempting to steal or alter patient data. PKI enhances EHR security by providing cryptographic protections that ensure data remains confidential, authentic, and tamper-proof.

User Authentication for EHR Access – PKI-based digital certificates replace traditional password authentication, preventing unauthorized users from accessing medical records.

Data Integrity with Digital Signatures – Healthcare providers digitally sign prescriptions, test results, and medical reports, ensuring that documents remain unaltered.

Secure Data Sharing – PKI encrypts EHR transmissions between hospitals, laboratories, insurance providers, and pharmacies, ensuring secure exchange of medical data.

PKI for Telemedicine and Remote Healthcare Services

Telemedicine has become a crucial component of modern healthcare, allowing remote consultations, digital prescriptions, and real-time patient monitoring. However, securing telemedicine platforms and protecting patient confidentiality is essential. PKI enhances telemedicine security by:

Authenticating Healthcare Providers – Digital certificates verify the identities of doctors, nurses, and telehealth practitioners, ensuring that only licensed professionals can access patient data.

Encrypting Video Consultations – Telemedicine platforms use TLS/SSL encryption to protect live video calls and online medical sessions from interception.

Digitally Signing Prescriptions – Doctors can sign e-prescriptions using PKI-based electronic signatures, ensuring authenticity and preventing prescription fraud.

PKI for Medical Device and IoMT Security

The rise of Internet of Medical Things (IoMT) devices, including smart insulin pumps, heart monitors, and MRI scanners, has improved patient care but also introduced security risks. If compromised, these devices could expose sensitive medical data or be manipulated to harm patients. PKI enhances medical device security by:

Authenticating Medical Devices – Digital certificates verify that only authorized devices can connect to hospital networks.

Encrypting Device Communications – PKI ensures that data transmitted between IoMT devices and healthcare systems remains confidential.

Firmware and Software Integrity – Medical device manufacturers use PKI-based code signing to ensure that only trusted firmware updates are installed.

PKI in Healthcare Identity and Access Management (IAM)

Identity and access management (IAM) is a critical aspect of healthcare cybersecurity. Healthcare professionals, patients, and third-party vendors require access to different medical systems, but unauthorized access must be prevented. PKI strengthens IAM in healthcare by:

Role-Based Access Control (RBAC) – Digital certificates grant access based on user roles, ensuring that only doctors, nurses, or administrators can view specific patient records.

Single Sign-On (SSO) for Healthcare Portals – PKI enables SSO solutions, allowing users to access multiple healthcare applications with a single, secure authentication.

Federated Identity Management – PKI allows secure authentication across different healthcare organizations, enabling seamless access to patient records, insurance claims, and laboratory data.

PKI for Healthcare Email and Communication Security

Healthcare organizations exchange sensitive information via email, faxes, and digital messages, making communication security a top priority. PKI enhances secure communication by:

S/MIME Email Encryption – Hospitals and clinics use S/MIME (Secure/Multipurpose Internet Mail Extensions) to encrypt and digitally sign emails, preventing phishing and email spoofing attacks.

Secure Messaging for Medical Professionals – PKI protects instant messaging between doctors, nurses, and pharmacists, ensuring confidential discussions about patient care.

Digital Signatures for Medical Reports – Healthcare professionals digitally sign medical reports, discharge summaries, and insurance claims, ensuring authenticity and non-repudiation.

Regulatory Compliance and Legal Requirements

The healthcare industry is subject to strict data protection laws and compliance requirements that mandate secure handling of patient data. PKI helps healthcare organizations comply with:

HIPAA (Health Insurance Portability and Accountability Act) – Requires strong encryption and authentication for electronic patient records and medical communications.

GDPR (General Data Protection Regulation) – Mandates end-to-end encryption and access controls for European healthcare providers handling patient data.

HITECH Act – Encourages electronic health information exchange while ensuring that healthcare data is secure and compliant.

Challenges of Implementing PKI in Healthcare

Despite its benefits, implementing PKI in healthcare environments presents challenges:

Complexity of Certificate Management – Healthcare organizations must manage thousands of digital certificates for EHR systems, medical devices, and staff authentication.

Integration with Legacy Systems – Many hospitals still rely on legacy IT infrastructure that lacks built-in PKI support.

User Training and Adoption – Healthcare providers may be unfamiliar with PKI-based authentication, requiring training to use digital certificates effectively.

Scalability for Large Health Networks – Large hospitals and national health systems require cloud-based PKI solutions that can scale efficiently.

Future Trends in PKI and Healthcare Security

As technology advances, PKI will continue to play a crucial role in healthcare cybersecurity. Emerging trends include:

Blockchain-Based Medical Record Security – Some healthcare providers are exploring blockchain-integrated PKI to ensure immutable patient records and prevent data tampering.

Post-Quantum Cryptography (PQC) in Healthcare – Quantum-resistant cryptographic algorithms will be integrated into PKI for future-proofed medical data security.

Artificial Intelligence for PKI Monitoring – AI-driven security systems will enhance PKI-based threat detection, preventing unauthorized access to healthcare data.

Decentralized Digital Identity in Healthcare – Patients may soon use self-sovereign digital IDs, secured by PKI, to access medical services across different providers.

PKI is essential for securing EHRs, medical devices, telemedicine, and healthcare communications. By integrating certificate-based authentication, encryption, and digital signatures, healthcare organizations can protect patient privacy, prevent cyber threats, and ensure compliance with global data security regulations.

Risks and Threats in PKI Implementations

Public Key Infrastructure (PKI) is a critical component of cybersecurity, enabling secure authentication, encryption, and digital signatures. It is widely used across industries, including financial services, healthcare, government, and cloud computing, to protect sensitive data and digital identities. However, despite its strong security benefits, PKI is not immune to risks and vulnerabilities. Poor implementation, mismanagement, or evolving cyber threats can compromise the integrity of a PKI system. Organizations relying on PKI must be aware of these risks and take proactive measures to mitigate them.

Private Key Compromise

The security of PKI is fundamentally dependent on private keys, which must remain confidential and protected at all times. If a private key is compromised, attackers can impersonate users, decrypt sensitive data, or issue fraudulent certificates. Private key compromise can occur due to:

Weak Key Storage – If private keys are stored in insecure locations, such as unprotected files or software-based keystores, they are vulnerable to theft.

Malware and Keyloggers – Attackers use malware to extract cryptographic keys from compromised systems.

Insider Threats – Employees with access to PKI systems may steal or misuse private keys for malicious purposes.

Inadequate Hardware Security – Without Hardware Security Modules (HSMs) or Trusted Platform Modules (TPMs), private keys are more susceptible to theft.

Certificate Misuse and Fraudulent Certificates

Attackers can exploit weaknesses in PKI to issue or obtain fraudulent certificates, allowing them to conduct man-in-the-middle (MITM) attacks, phishing campaigns, or website impersonation. Risks related to certificate misuse include:

Compromised Certificate Authorities (CAs) – If a CA's private key is compromised, attackers can issue trusted certificates for malicious purposes.

Misissued Certificates – Errors or policy violations by CAs can lead to certificates being issued to unauthorized entities.

Rogue or Untrusted CAs – Some organizations unknowingly trust illegitimate or unauthorized CAs, exposing themselves to potential security breaches.

Expired or Revoked Certificates Still in Use – Failure to revoke compromised certificates allows attackers to exploit them indefinitely.

Weak Cryptographic Algorithms and Key Lengths

PKI security relies on strong cryptographic algorithms to protect digital identities and encrypt communications. However, outdated or weak cryptographic methods pose a significant risk. Threats include:

Use of Deprecated Algorithms – Algorithms like SHA-1 and MD5 are no longer considered secure and should be replaced with SHA-256 or higher.

Short Key Lengths – Keys shorter than 2048-bit RSA or 256-bit ECC can be cracked with brute-force attacks.

Quantum Computing Threats – Future quantum computers may break existing asymmetric cryptographic algorithms, requiring a transition to post-quantum cryptography (PQC).

Man-in-the-Middle (MITM) Attacks

In MITM attacks, an attacker intercepts communication between two parties to eavesdrop or manipulate data. If PKI is not properly implemented, attackers can exploit weaknesses to perform MITM attacks using:

Stolen or Forged Certificates – Attackers use fraudulent certificates to impersonate legitimate entities.

DNS Spoofing and SSL Stripping – Manipulating domain name resolution or forcing downgraded encryption can allow attackers to intercept encrypted traffic.

Weak Authentication in TLS/SSL Handshakes – Failing to verify digital certificates properly can lead to spoofed connections.

Certificate Revocation Challenges

Revoking compromised or outdated certificates is crucial for maintaining PKI security. However, organizations often face challenges in effectively revoking certificates, leading to:

Delayed Revocation Processing – Revoked certificates may remain trusted if revocation lists are not updated frequently.

Inefficient Certificate Revocation Lists (CRLs) – Large CRLs can slow down authentication processes, leading to performance issues.

Weak OCSP Implementations – If Online Certificate Status Protocol (OCSP) servers fail, systems may be unable to verify certificate validity in real time.

Human Errors and Misconfigurations

PKI is complex, and improper configurations can introduce security vulnerabilities. Common human errors in PKI implementations include:

Improper Certificate Authority (CA) Hierarchies – Incorrectly setting up root and intermediate CAs can lead to trust issues and security gaps.

Failure to Rotate Keys and Certificates – Organizations that reuse old certificates or fail to renew them on time risk security breaches.

Misconfigured TLS Settings – Enabling obsolete protocols (SSLv3, TLS 1.0) exposes systems to attacks such as BEAST and POODLE.

Weak Certificate Policies – Allowing certificates with long validity periods (5+ years) increases exposure to compromise.

Scalability and Certificate Management Issues

As organizations scale, managing thousands to millions of digital certificates becomes increasingly difficult. Common challenges include:

Lack of Centralized Certificate Management – Without a Certificate Management System (CMS), organizations struggle to track, renew, or revoke certificates.

Expired Certificates Causing System Failures – Many high-profile system outages have occurred due to expired certificates disrupting critical services.

Certificate Sprawl – Organizations using multiple PKI providers may have difficulty maintaining visibility over all issued certificates.

Supply Chain and Third-Party Risks

Organizations rely on third-party vendors, cloud services, and external CAs for PKI management. However, weaknesses in the supply chain introduce risks:

Third-Party CA Breaches – If an external CA is compromised, all organizations trusting its certificates are affected.

Compromised IoT and Embedded Devices – Many IoT manufacturers fail to secure PKI implementations, leading to widespread vulnerabilities.

Weak Trust in Cloud-Based PKI Services – Some cloud-based PKI providers do not offer strong key protection mechanisms, increasing the risk of key exposure.

Defending Against PKI Risks and Threats

Organizations can mitigate PKI risks by implementing best practices, including:

Enforcing Strong Cryptography – Use RSA 4096-bit or ECC 384-bit for long-term security. Transition to post-quantum cryptography (PQC) to future-proof PKI systems.

Using Hardware Security Modules (HSMs) – Store private keys in tamper-proof HSMs to prevent key theft and unauthorized access.

Implementing Automated Certificate Management – Use certificate lifecycle management tools to prevent expired certificates, weak keys, and misconfigurations.

Enabling OCSP Stapling – Reduce reliance on Certificate Revocation Lists (CRLs) by enabling real-time certificate status verification.

Enforcing Multi-Factor Authentication (MFA) for CA Administrators – Require MFA to prevent unauthorized access to PKI administration consoles.

Regular PKI Audits and Compliance Checks – Conduct annual security audits to identify weaknesses and ensure compliance with NIST, ISO 27001, PCI DSS, and GDPR.

Monitoring for Anomalous PKI Activity – Use AI-driven security analytics to detect unusual certificate issuance, revocation requests, or key access patterns.

PKI remains one of the strongest security frameworks available, but its effectiveness depends on careful implementation, continuous monitoring, and proactive security measures. Organizations must stay ahead of emerging threats, cryptographic advancements, and regulatory requirements to maintain a secure and reliable PKI infrastructure.

Common PKI Vulnerabilities and How to Mitigate Them

Public Key Infrastructure (PKI) is a foundational security framework used to protect digital identities, enable encryption, and ensure data integrity across various industries. However, despite its strength, PKI implementations can be vulnerable to misconfigurations, weak cryptographic practices, and evolving cyber threats. Attackers continuously exploit weaknesses in certificate management, key storage, and authentication mechanisms to bypass security controls. Organizations must be aware of these vulnerabilities and implement effective mitigation strategies to maintain a secure and resilient PKI environment.

Weak Key Management and Private Key Exposure

One of the most critical vulnerabilities in PKI is the compromise of private keys, which are used to sign digital certificates and decrypt sensitive information. If a private key is exposed, attackers can impersonate trusted entities, decrypt communications, or issue fraudulent certificates.

Causes:

Improper key storage – Storing private keys in unencrypted files or software-based keystores makes them susceptible to theft.

Shared key usage – Using the same private key for multiple applications increases the risk of compromise.

Lack of key rotation – Failing to change private keys regularly makes them vulnerable to long-term attacks.

Mitigation Strategies:

Use Hardware Security Modules (HSMs) to store private keys securely and prevent unauthorized access.

Implement key rotation policies that mandate periodic updates of cryptographic keys.

Restrict access to private keys using role-based access control (RBAC) and multi-factor authentication (MFA).

Use Elliptic Curve Cryptography (ECC) or RSA with key lengths of at least 2048 bits to strengthen cryptographic security.

Certificate Authority (CA) Compromise

A compromised Certificate Authority (CA) is one of the most severe PKI vulnerabilities, as attackers can issue fraudulent certificates to impersonate legitimate entities. CA breaches allow hackers to perform man-in-the-middle (MITM) attacks, phishing campaigns, and unauthorized decryption of sensitive data.

Causes:

Weak security controls in CAs – Poorly protected CA infrastructure can be exploited by attackers.

Malware or insider threats – Malicious insiders or malware can steal CA credentials and issue unauthorized certificates.

Over-reliance on a single CA – If a CA is breached, all certificates issued by it are at risk.

Mitigation Strategies:

Use multi-tiered CA hierarchies with separate root and intermediate CAs to reduce the impact of a compromise.

Implement strict access controls and monitoring for CA administrators to prevent insider threats.

Regularly audit and test CA security to detect vulnerabilities before they can be exploited.

Require certificate transparency logs to track and verify all issued certificates.

Expired or Unrevoked Certificates

Certificates that are expired or not properly revoked can expose organizations to security risks, such as system failures and unauthorized access. Attackers can exploit old or compromised certificates if they remain valid beyond their intended lifespan.

Causes:

Lack of centralized certificate management – Organizations with many certificates may lose track of expiration dates.

Failure to revoke compromised certificates – If a certificate is not revoked after a security breach, attackers can continue using it.

Manual renewal processes – Manually tracking certificate renewals increases the risk of oversight.

Mitigation Strategies:

Deploy Automated Certificate Management (ACM) systems to track, renew, and revoke certificates efficiently.

Use Online Certificate Status Protocol (OCSP) stapling to validate certificate revocation status in real time.

Enforce policies requiring short-lived certificates to reduce the risk of outdated credentials.

Man-in-the-Middle (MITM) Attacks Due to Weak Validation

MITM attacks occur when an attacker intercepts and alters communications between two parties. PKI can be exploited in MITM attacks if certificate validation is weak or improperly implemented.

Causes:

Failure to validate certificate chains – Allowing certificates from unknown or untrusted CAs can introduce security risks.

Use of deprecated protocols – Supporting outdated encryption protocols, such as SSL 3.0 or TLS 1.0, increases vulnerability to MITM attacks.

Accepting self-signed certificates – Trusting self-signed certificates without proper validation exposes systems to impersonation attacks.

Mitigation Strategies:

Enforce strict certificate validation policies, ensuring that certificates are issued by trusted CAs.

Disable support for weak encryption protocols and enforce TLS 1.2 or higher.

Use mutual TLS (mTLS) to authenticate both clients and servers in sensitive transactions.

Vulnerabilities in Cryptographic Algorithms

PKI security is based on strong cryptographic algorithms, but as computing power increases, older algorithms become vulnerable to brute-force attacks and cryptanalysis. Weak algorithms can compromise encryption, digital signatures, and authentication mechanisms.

Causes:

Use of outdated hashing algorithms (e.g., MD5, SHA-1) that are susceptible to collisions.

Short encryption key lengths that can be broken using brute-force attacks.

Emerging quantum computing threats that could render current asymmetric encryption ineffective.

Mitigation Strategies:

Migrate to SHA-256 or stronger hashing algorithms.

Use RSA-4096, ECC-384, or higher key lengths for encryption and signing.

Prepare for post-quantum cryptography (PQC) by exploring quantum-resistant algorithms.

Certificate Spoofing and Fraudulent Certificates

Attackers can create fraudulent certificates to impersonate legitimate websites, tricking users into revealing sensitive information. Spoofing PKI certificates can lead to phishing attacks, data breaches, and unauthorized system access.

Causes:

Domain Validation (DV) certificate exploitation – Some attackers trick CAs into issuing certificates for fake or typo-squatted domains.

Compromised CA infrastructure – If a CA's system is hacked, fraudulent certificates can be issued.

Weak certificate verification – Users and applications may fail to properly verify digital signatures.

Mitigation Strategies:

Implement Extended Validation (EV) certificates for high-security applications to provide stronger identity verification.

Enforce Certificate Transparency (CT) logs to detect and prevent fraudulent certificate issuance.

Require multi-factor authentication (MFA) for CA administrators to prevent unauthorized certificate issuance.

Lack of PKI Monitoring and Incident Response

Many organizations do not have proper monitoring and incident response strategies for PKI-related security events. Without real-time detection, malicious activities may go unnoticed for extended periods.

Causes:

Lack of continuous PKI auditing – Organizations fail to track certificate usage, revocations, and key access.

Slow response to PKI-related incidents – Without automated alerts, responding to threats takes too long.

Inadequate logging mechanisms – If PKI activities are not logged, forensic investigations become difficult.

Mitigation Strategies:

Deploy Security Information and Event Management (SIEM) systems to monitor PKI activity in real time.

Automate PKI logging and auditing to detect anomalies and unauthorized certificate issuance.

Implement AI-driven threat detection to identify potential PKI-based attacks before they escalate.

PKI remains one of the most powerful security frameworks, but improper implementation and management introduce significant risks. Organizations must adopt strong key management, automated certificate renewal, continuous monitoring, and cryptographic best practices to mitigate PKI vulnerabilities and maintain a resilient security infrastructure.

Quantum Computing and the Future of PKI

Quantum computing represents one of the most significant advancements in computational technology, promising exponential improvements in processing power and problem-solving capabilities. While this innovation has the potential to revolutionize various industries, it also poses a major threat to current cryptographic systems, including Public Key Infrastructure (PKI). As quantum computers evolve, they will be capable of breaking widely used encryption algorithms, forcing organizations to transition to post-quantum cryptography (PQC) to maintain security. Understanding the impact of quantum computing on PKI and preparing for quantum-resistant security models is critical for governments, enterprises, and cybersecurity professionals.

The Threat of Quantum Computing to PKI

PKI relies on asymmetric cryptographic algorithms for key exchange, digital signatures, and certificate-based authentication. The security of these algorithms is based on the difficulty of solving mathematical problems such as integer factorization (RSA) and discrete logarithms (ECC, DSA, DH). Traditional computers cannot efficiently solve these problems within a reasonable timeframe, making modern cryptographic systems secure. However, quantum computers leverage quantum superposition and entanglement, allowing them to perform calculations that are infeasible for classical computers.

One of the most critical quantum computing algorithms threatening PKI is Shor's Algorithm, which can efficiently factor large numbers and compute discrete logarithms. This means that widely used RSA, ECC (Elliptic Curve Cryptography), and DSA (Digital Signature Algorithm) will become vulnerable to quantum attacks once sufficiently powerful quantum computers are developed. If an attacker can break these encryption schemes, they can:

Decrypt sensitive communications protected by TLS/SSL certificates.

Forge digital signatures, impersonating trusted entities in PKI-based authentication systems.

Compromise VPNs and secure tunnels that rely on RSA or ECC for key exchange.

Access encrypted financial, healthcare, and government data, threatening privacy and national security.

Post-Quantum Cryptography (PQC) and the Future of PKI

To defend against quantum threats, researchers and cryptographers are developing post-quantum cryptographic (PQC) algorithms, which are designed to be resistant to quantum attacks. These algorithms do not rely on integer factorization or discrete logarithm problems and instead use alternative mathematical approaches that quantum computers cannot easily solve.

The National Institute of Standards and Technology (NIST) has been leading the effort to standardize post-quantum cryptographic algorithms. Some of the most promising PQC algorithms include:

Lattice-Based Cryptography – Relies on the complexity of solving lattice problems, which remain difficult for quantum computers. Examples include Kyber (for key exchange) and Dilithium (for digital signatures).

Hash-Based Cryptography – Uses hash functions to create quantum-safe digital signatures, such as SPHINCS+.

Code-Based Cryptography – Based on error-correcting codes, such as Classic McEliece, which has been studied for decades and remains secure against quantum attacks.

Multivariate Polynomial Cryptography – Relies on solving systems of multivariate equations, offering a different approach to quantum-resistant encryption.

The integration of PQC into PKI systems will require migrating certificate authorities (CAs), digital signatures, and encrypted communications to quantum-resistant cryptographic standards. Organizations must begin assessing their PKI infrastructure and planning for the transition to PQC to ensure future security.

Challenges of Transitioning PKI to Quantum-Safe Cryptography

While PQC offers a solution to quantum threats, transitioning from classical PKI to quantum-resistant PKI introduces several challenges:

Backward Compatibility Issues

Existing systems rely on RSA and ECC-based digital certificates. Transitioning to PQC will require dual-mode encryption, where both classical and quantum-safe algorithms operate simultaneously until full migration is complete.

Legacy applications and devices may not support PQC algorithms, requiring updates or replacements.

Increased Computational Overhead

Many PQC algorithms require larger key sizes and signatures than traditional RSA and ECC, increasing computational demands.

Secure communication protocols, such as TLS 1.3, must be modified to incorporate quantum-resistant key exchange methods.

Certificate Authority (CA) Adaptation

PKI ecosystems depend on certificate authorities (CAs) to issue and validate digital certificates. CAs must integrate PQC-based certificates and develop hybrid certificate chains that support both classical and post-quantum algorithms.

Key Management and Infrastructure Upgrades

Organizations must update their hardware security modules (HSMs), key management systems (KMS), and cryptographic libraries to support PQC.

Secure storage and transfer of larger cryptographic keys will require optimization to minimize performance degradation.

Uncertainty in Algorithm Selection

While NIST is finalizing post-quantum cryptographic standards, there is still uncertainty about which algorithms will be widely adopted.

Organizations must remain flexible and prepare for future cryptographic changes as new quantum-safe techniques are developed.

Steps to Prepare for Post-Quantum PKI

Organizations must proactively plan for the quantum era by assessing their PKI infrastructure and implementing transition strategies. Key steps include:

Identifying Quantum-Vulnerable Cryptography – Organizations should conduct cryptographic inventories to determine where RSA, ECC, and other quantum-susceptible algorithms are used.

Implementing Hybrid Cryptographic Solutions – Many security experts recommend using hybrid cryptography, where both classical and post-quantum algorithms are used together during the transition phase.

Upgrading Digital Certificates and CA Infrastructure – CAs must begin issuing quantum-resistant certificates and adopting PQC-supported digital signature algorithms.

Testing PQC Algorithms in Secure Environments – Organizations should experiment with post-quantum cryptographic libraries in test environments before full deployment.

Ensuring Compliance with Emerging Standards – Regulatory agencies and cybersecurity frameworks will mandate quantum-resistant encryption in critical industries. Enterprises must stay updated with NIST, ISO, and industry-specific guidelines.

Quantum-Safe PKI in the Future

The future of PKI in the quantum era will involve continuous adaptation to new cryptographic threats. Some emerging trends in quantum-safe PKI include:

Quantum Key Distribution (QKD) – A technique using quantum mechanics to distribute encryption keys securely. While still experimental, QKD has the potential to replace classical key exchange mechanisms in high-security environments.

Blockchain and Decentralized PKI (dPKI) – Some researchers are exploring blockchain-based PKI to enhance trust and security in quantum-resistant identity verification.

Artificial Intelligence for PKI Monitoring – AI-powered security analytics may help detect quantum-based cyber threats and prevent cryptographic attacks.

Government-Led Quantum Security Initiatives – Governments worldwide are investing in quantum cybersecurity research, establishing frameworks to secure national infrastructure against quantum adversaries.

While large-scale quantum computers capable of breaking PKI algorithms are still years away, organizations must act now to future-proof their encryption systems. Transitioning to post-quantum PKI will require careful planning, investment in new cryptographic technologies, and adherence to emerging security standards. As quantum computing continues to evolve, staying ahead of cryptographic threats will be essential to maintaining trust and security in the digital world.

PKI Compliance and Regulatory Requirements

Public Key Infrastructure (PKI) plays a crucial role in securing digital transactions, protecting sensitive data, and ensuring the authenticity of users and devices. However, organizations that implement PKI must adhere to strict compliance and regulatory requirements to maintain trust, security, and legal validity. Various industries and governments worldwide enforce standards, laws, and best practices to ensure that PKI is implemented securely and effectively. Failure to comply with these regulations can result in legal consequences, data breaches, and financial penalties. Understanding PKI compliance requirements is essential for organizations operating in financial services, healthcare, government, and cloud computing.

The Importance of PKI Compliance

PKI compliance ensures that digital certificates, encryption methods, and authentication protocols meet industry standards and legal regulations. Compliance is necessary for:

Ensuring Trust – Certificates issued by trusted Certificate Authorities (CAs) must meet recognized standards to be accepted by browsers, operating systems, and cloud services.

Preventing Data Breaches – Regulatory frameworks mandate the use of encryption and access controls to protect sensitive information from unauthorized access.

Enforcing Security Policies – Organizations must follow certificate lifecycle management policies to prevent expired, weak, or compromised certificates from being used.

Legal and Contractual Requirements – Digital signatures, secure email communications, and encrypted transactions must comply with international legal frameworks to be recognized as valid.

Key Regulations and Standards Governing PKI

1. eIDAS (Electronic Identification, Authentication and Trust Services) – European Union

The eIDAS Regulation (EU 910/2014) establishes the legal framework for electronic signatures, trust services, and digital certificates within the European Union. It ensures that electronic transactions are legally binding and recognized across EU member states.

Qualified Electronic Signatures (QES) – eIDAS defines Qualified Electronic Signatures as the most secure type of digital signature, requiring PKI-backed certificates issued by Qualified Trust Service Providers (QTSPs).

Timestamping Services – Digital certificates must include trusted timestamps to ensure document authenticity and prevent backdating.

eSeals for Businesses – Organizations must use digital certificates for electronic seals (eSeals) to authenticate documents and transactions legally.

2. HIPAA (Health Insurance Portability and Accountability Act) – United States

HIPAA mandates strong encryption and authentication mechanisms for protecting electronic Protected Health Information (ePHI) in the healthcare sector. PKI plays a key role in securing healthcare data, electronic health records (EHRs), and medical device communications.

Data Encryption – Healthcare organizations must encrypt ePHI during storage and transmission using PKI-based security controls.

Digital Signatures – PKI ensures document integrity and compliance with HIPAA's Security Rule by providing tamper-proof medical records and prescriptions.

Identity and Access Management – Digital certificates help authenticate healthcare providers and patients before accessing sensitive medical data.

3. PCI DSS (Payment Card Industry Data Security Standard) – Financial Services

PCI DSS establishes security requirements for financial institutions, credit card companies, and payment service providers. PKI is essential for securing online transactions, payment processing, and customer authentication.

TLS/SSL Certificates – Financial institutions must use trusted TLS/SSL certificates to encrypt payment transactions and prevent data breaches.

Secure Customer Authentication (SCA) – PKI enables two-factor authentication (2FA) and digital signatures to prevent payment fraud.

Digital Certificate Management – Organizations must track, renew, and revoke certificates to maintain compliance and prevent security gaps.

4. FIPS 140-2 / FIPS 140-3 (Federal Information Processing Standards) – United States Government

The FIPS 140-2 / 140-3 standards, established by the National Institute of Standards and Technology (NIST), define cryptographic module security requirements for U.S. federal agencies and contractors. PKI implementations used in government and defense sectors must comply with FIPS regulations.

Hardware Security Modules (HSMs) – FIPS-compliant organizations must store private keys in FIPS 140-2 Level 3 or higher HSMs to prevent unauthorized access.

Strong Cryptographic Algorithms – The use of RSA-2048+, ECC-384, or SHA-256+ is required to meet federal security standards.

Certificate-Based Authentication – Government employees must use PKI smart cards for secure access to federal systems and networks.

5. NIST SP 800-57 & NIST SP 800-63 – United States Cybersecurity Standards

NIST provides guidelines for cryptographic key management and digital identity authentication in PKI environments. Organizations in defense, critical infrastructure, and cloud services must comply with these standards.

Key Management Requirements – Organizations must implement automated key rotation, revocation, and expiration policies to reduce the risk of key compromise.

Digital Identity Assurance – NIST SP 800-63 defines identity assurance levels (IALs) that require PKI-based authentication for high-security applications.

Best Practices for PKI Compliance

Organizations must implement best practices for PKI governance and security to remain compliant with regulatory frameworks.

Use Trusted Certificate Authorities (CAs) – Certificates must be issued by recognized and compliant CAs to maintain trust.

Implement Certificate Lifecycle Management (CLM) – Automate certificate issuance, renewal, and revocation to prevent service disruptions.

Maintain Secure Key Storage – Use HSMs, Trusted Platform Modules (TPMs), or cloud-based key management systems to protect private keys.

Regular PKI Audits and Compliance Reviews – Conduct annual security audits to detect vulnerabilities and verify compliance with ISO 27001, NIST, and industry-specific regulations.

Enable OCSP and Certificate Transparency Logs – Organizations must implement real-time certificate validation to detect fraudulent certificates and prevent security incidents.

Challenges in PKI Compliance

Despite its security benefits, achieving full PKI compliance presents challenges:

Complex Regulatory Landscape – Organizations operating in multiple jurisdictions must navigate overlapping security laws and certification requirements.

Certificate Sprawl and Management Overhead – Large enterprises may struggle to track and manage thousands of certificates across systems and devices.

Legacy System Integration – Many businesses still rely on legacy applications that do not support modern PKI standards, requiring system upgrades.

Scalability in Cloud and IoT Environments – Cloud services and IoT device authentication require highly scalable PKI infrastructures that comply with industry regulations.

The Future of PKI Compliance

As cybersecurity threats evolve, PKI compliance requirements will continue to adapt. Emerging trends in PKI compliance include:

Post-Quantum Cryptography (PQC) Compliance – Governments and organizations will need to transition to quantum-resistant encryption standards as quantum computing threats emerge.

Blockchain and Decentralized PKI (dPKI) – Regulatory bodies may explore blockchain-based digital identity verification for secure certificate issuance and trust management.

Artificial Intelligence for Compliance Monitoring – AI-driven threat detection and compliance automation will enhance PKI governance and regulatory enforcement.

PKI compliance is essential for maintaining trust, security, and legal recognition in digital transactions. Organizations must continuously monitor evolving regulatory requirements, update cryptographic policies, and implement best practices to ensure a secure and compliant PKI infrastructure.

Best Practices for Secure PKI Deployment

Public Key Infrastructure (PKI) is a critical component of modern cybersecurity, providing encryption, authentication, and digital signatures to protect sensitive data and ensure the integrity of online transactions. However, the security of a PKI system is only as strong as its implementation. Poorly managed PKI deployments can introduce vulnerabilities, leading to data breaches, certificate misuse, and unauthorized access. To maximize security and maintain trust, organizations must follow best practices for PKI deployment, covering certificate authority (CA) management, key protection, certificate lifecycle management, and compliance with industry standards.

Establishing a Secure Certificate Authority (CA) Infrastructure

A Certificate Authority (CA) is the core of any PKI system, issuing and managing digital certificates. If a CA is compromised, attackers can generate fraudulent certificates, impersonate legitimate entities, or decrypt encrypted communications. Securing the CA infrastructure is a top priority in any PKI deployment.

Use a Multi-Tier CA Hierarchy – Implement a Root CA with one or more Intermediate CAs to improve security. The Root CA should be offline to reduce the risk of compromise, while the Intermediate CAs handle day-to-day certificate issuance.

Protect Root and Intermediate CA Private Keys – Store private keys in Hardware Security Modules (HSMs) that meet FIPS 140-2 Level 3 or higher standards to prevent unauthorized access.

Enforce Strict CA Access Controls – Restrict administrative access to CA servers using role-based access control (RBAC), multi-factor authentication (MFA), and physical security measures.

Perform Regular CA Audits – Conduct periodic security audits and compliance reviews to verify CA integrity and detect potential security weaknesses.

Implementing Strong Cryptographic Standards

PKI security relies on cryptographic algorithms to protect certificates and secure communication channels. Organizations must use strong encryption standards and regularly update their cryptographic policies to defend against evolving threats.

Use Strong Key Lengths – Implement RSA 4096-bit, ECC 384-bit, or higher key lengths for secure encryption and digital signatures.

Adopt Post-Quantum Cryptography (PQC) Readiness – Begin planning for a transition to quantum-resistant algorithms, such as lattice-based and hash-based cryptography, as quantum computing evolves.

Ensure Secure Hashing Algorithms – Use SHA-256, SHA-384, or SHA-512 for digital signatures to prevent collision attacks. Avoid deprecated algorithms like SHA-1 and MD5.

Enable Perfect Forward Secrecy (PFS) – Configure TLS implementations to use ephemeral key exchanges, such as ECDHE (Elliptic Curve Diffie-Hellman Ephemeral), to protect past communications in case private keys are compromised.

Securing Private Key Storage and Management

Private keys are the most sensitive assets in a PKI deployment. If exposed, attackers can forge digital signatures or decrypt encrypted communications. Organizations must follow best practices to store, protect, and manage private keys securely.

Use HSMs for Secure Key Storage – Store private keys in HSMs, TPMs (Trusted Platform Modules), or cloud-based key management systems (KMS) to prevent unauthorized access.

Implement Key Rotation Policies – Periodically rotate cryptographic keys to minimize the impact of potential key compromises.

Enforce Secure Key Backup Procedures – Back up private keys securely in encrypted storage, ensuring that only authorized personnel can access them.

Monitor and Restrict Key Access – Log all access attempts to cryptographic keys and enforce principle of least privilege (PoLP) to prevent misuse.

Managing Certificate Lifecycle Effectively

Poor certificate lifecycle management can lead to security gaps, service disruptions, and compliance violations. Organizations must track and manage the entire lifecycle of digital certificates, from issuance to expiration and revocation.

Automate Certificate Issuance and Renewal – Use a Certificate Management System (CMS) or Automated Certificate Management Environment (ACME) to prevent expired certificates from disrupting business operations.

Set Short Expiry Periods for Certificates – Use shorter certificate lifetimes (1 year or less) to reduce the risk of long-term key exposure.

Monitor Expiring Certificates – Implement real-time monitoring and alerting systems to track expiring certificates and ensure timely renewal.

Revoke Compromised Certificates Immediately – Implement Certificate Revocation Lists (CRLs) and Online Certificate Status Protocol (OCSP) for real-time certificate validation.

Configuring Secure TLS and SSL Implementations

PKI secures Transport Layer Security (TLS) and Secure Sockets Layer (SSL) protocols, which protect online transactions, cloud services, and enterprise networks. Misconfigured TLS settings can expose systems to man-in-the-middle (MITM) attacks and downgrade attacks.

Disable Weak Protocols – Enforce TLS 1.2 or higher and disable outdated versions such as SSL 3.0, TLS 1.0, and TLS 1.1.

Use Strong Cipher Suites – Restrict the use of weak encryption ciphers and enable AES-GCM, ChaCha20, and ECDHE key exchange mechanisms.

Implement Mutual TLS (mTLS) – Require certificate-based authentication for both clients and servers in high-security environments.

Implementing Robust Access Controls and Monitoring

Unauthorized access to PKI systems can lead to certificate misuse, key theft, and operational disruptions. Organizations must implement strong identity and access management (IAM) policies to protect PKI resources.

Enforce Multi-Factor Authentication (MFA) – Require MFA for CA administrators, PKI operators, and certificate requestors to prevent unauthorized access.

Use Role-Based Access Control (RBAC) – Assign PKI roles with least privilege permissions, ensuring that only authorized personnel can issue, revoke, or modify certificates.

Log and Monitor PKI Activity – Use Security Information and Event Management (SIEM) solutions to monitor PKI-related logs, detect anomalies, and prevent insider threats.

Ensuring Compliance with Regulatory Standards

PKI implementations must align with industry regulations and security frameworks to ensure legal compliance and prevent data breaches. Different industries have specific compliance requirements for digital certificates and encryption.

Follow eIDAS Guidelines for Digital Signatures – In the EU, PKI deployments must comply with eIDAS (Electronic Identification,

Authentication and Trust Services) for legally recognized digital signatures.

Ensure HIPAA Compliance for Healthcare – Healthcare providers must secure electronic health records (EHRs) and patient data using PKI-backed encryption and authentication.

Meet PCI DSS Requirements for Financial Transactions – Financial institutions must use TLS encryption and certificate-based authentication to protect credit card transactions and online payments.

Adopt NIST 800-57 Key Management Guidelines – Organizations following U.S. government cybersecurity standards must adhere to NIST recommendations for cryptographic key lifecycle management.

Preparing for the Future of PKI

The future of PKI will be shaped by emerging threats, technological advancements, and evolving security frameworks. Organizations must proactively adapt their PKI infrastructure to remain resilient against modern cybersecurity challenges.

Transition to Post-Quantum Cryptography (PQC) – Begin planning for quantum-resistant cryptographic algorithms as quantum computing advances.

Adopt Decentralized PKI (dPKI) – Blockchain-based decentralized PKI may provide tamper-proof digital identity verification for next-generation authentication systems.

Enhance AI-Driven PKI Security – Artificial intelligence and machine learning will play a role in automating threat detection and anomaly analysis in PKI environments.

PKI is a cornerstone of modern cybersecurity, but its effectiveness depends on proper implementation, secure key management, and ongoing monitoring. By following best practices for secure PKI deployment, organizations can safeguard digital identities, communications, and critical infrastructure against evolving cyber threats.

Automating Certificate Management

Managing digital certificates is a fundamental aspect of Public Key Infrastructure (PKI) that ensures the security of encrypted communications, user authentication, and digital signatures. However, as organizations grow and adopt more digital services, the number of certificates they must manage increases exponentially. Manual certificate management introduces risks such as expired certificates, misconfigurations, security gaps, and operational inefficiencies. Automating certificate management streamlines the issuance, renewal, revocation, and monitoring of certificates, reducing human errors and strengthening security posture.

The Need for Automated Certificate Management

Organizations use PKI certificates for securing websites, cloud applications, IoT devices, enterprise networks, and financial transactions. However, certificate management becomes complex due to:

Increasing Number of Certificates – Enterprises manage thousands of certificates across different environments, including TLS/SSL, email encryption, VPN authentication, and IoT security.

Shorter Certificate Lifespans – Industry best practices recommend shorter certificate validity periods (e.g., 398 days for TLS certificates), increasing the frequency of renewals.

Compliance and Security Risks – Expired or compromised certificates can cause system outages, data breaches, and compliance violations with regulations such as PCI DSS, HIPAA, and GDPR.

Manual Renewal Challenges – Keeping track of expiration dates and manually renewing certificates increases administrative workload and introduces delays.

Automating certificate management addresses these challenges by ensuring timely issuance, renewal, revocation, and monitoring, reducing operational overhead while improving security.

Key Features of Automated Certificate Management

Automated certificate management solutions provide organizations with centralized control, real-time monitoring, and seamless integration with PKI environments. Key features include:

Automated Certificate Issuance – Certificates are issued instantly without manual intervention, ensuring fast deployment of new applications and services.

Automated Renewal and Replacement – Certificates are renewed before expiration, preventing disruptions and security risks.

Certificate Revocation and Lifecycle Management – Automates the process of revoking compromised or unused certificates and updating revocation lists.

Real-Time Monitoring and Alerts – Provides visibility into certificate health, sending alerts for expiring, revoked, or misconfigured certificates.

Policy Enforcement and Compliance Tracking – Ensures that all certificates comply with industry standards, internal security policies, and regulatory requirements.

Protocols and Tools for Automated Certificate Management

Several protocols and tools are used to automate certificate management in enterprise environments:

1. Automated Certificate Management Environment (ACME)

The ACME protocol is widely used for automated certificate issuance, renewal, and revocation. It was originally developed by the Internet Security Research Group (ISRG) for Let's Encrypt and is now supported by many certificate authorities (CAs).

How ACME Works:

The client requests a certificate from the ACME-compatible CA.

The CA verifies domain ownership automatically using HTTP, DNS, or TLS challenges.

Once verified, the certificate is issued and installed on the server.

The ACME client automatically renews the certificate before expiration.

Use Cases:

Automating TLS/SSL certificate issuance for web servers, cloud applications, and DevOps environments.

Securing load balancers, API gateways, and microservices in cloud-native applications.

2. Certificate Management Systems (CMS) and PKI Automation Tools

Many enterprises deploy Certificate Management Systems (CMS) to automate certificate handling across hybrid and multi-cloud environments. Popular tools include:

Venafi Trust Protection Platform – Provides enterprise-wide certificate lifecycle management, preventing outages and security risks.

DigiCert CertCentral – Automates certificate discovery, monitoring, and compliance enforcement.

Microsoft Active Directory Certificate Services (AD CS) – Integrates with Windows environments to automate enterprise certificate issuance and renewal.

AWS Certificate Manager (ACM) – Automates SSL/TLS certificate deployment for AWS services.

These platforms help automate large-scale certificate management, ensuring consistent security policies and compliance.

Benefits of Automating Certificate Management

Automating certificate management provides numerous security and operational advantages, helping organizations avoid common pitfalls associated with manual processes.

Eliminates Expired Certificate Risks – Prevents service outages, authentication failures, and security incidents caused by forgotten renewals.

Reduces Human Errors and Misconfigurations – Minimizes manual mistakes in certificate requests, issuance, and deployment.

Improves Security and Compliance – Ensures adherence to TLS best practices, regulatory requirements, and encryption standards.

Enhances Scalability for Cloud and DevOps – Automates certificate provisioning in dynamic, containerized, and multi-cloud environments.

Strengthens Incident Response and Risk Mitigation – Provides real-time alerts and automated revocation of compromised certificates.

Automating Certificate Renewal and Revocation

Certificate expiration can lead to critical failures in network authentication, encrypted communications, and application security. Automating renewals and revocations ensures continued trust in PKI-based authentication.

Automated Renewals:

Certificate management systems track expiration dates and renew certificates before they lapse.

Integration with ACME, enterprise CMS platforms, and cloud PKI services ensures seamless renewal processes.

Automated Revocation:

If a certificate is compromised, it must be revoked immediately. Automated systems update Certificate Revocation Lists (CRLs) and Online Certificate Status Protocol (OCSP) servers in real time.

Enterprises use automated revocation policies to disable misused, expired, or unauthorized certificates before they become security liabilities.

Challenges in Automating Certificate Management

Despite its advantages, automating certificate management comes with challenges:

Integration Complexity – Many organizations use legacy systems and multi-cloud environments that require extensive integration efforts.

Managing Certificate Sprawl – Enterprises with thousands of certificates must maintain visibility and prevent misconfigurations or unauthorized certificate issuance.

Ensuring Secure Key Management – Private key storage and lifecycle management must be carefully controlled to prevent compromise.

Compliance with Industry Standards – Organizations must continuously update cryptographic policies to align with evolving regulations such as NIST, PCI DSS, and eIDAS.

Best Practices for Implementing Automated Certificate Management

Organizations can maximize the benefits of automation by following best practices for certificate lifecycle management:

Deploy a Centralized Certificate Management System (CMS) – Use Venafi, DigiCert, AWS ACM, or Microsoft AD CS for enterprise-wide automation.

Use Short-Lived Certificates – Implement 90-day or 180-day certificate lifetimes to minimize long-term risks.

Monitor Certificates Continuously – Enable real-time logging, alerts, and anomaly detection for unauthorized or expired certificates.

Automate Key Rotation – Regularly rotate cryptographic keys to maintain security resilience.

Ensure Compliance with Cryptographic Standards – Adopt TLS 1.2 or higher, enforce SHA-256+ hashing, and use RSA-4096 or ECC-384 key lengths.

The Future of Automated Certificate Management

As cybersecurity threats evolve, organizations will continue to adopt advanced PKI automation technologies. Emerging trends include:

AI-Driven Certificate Management – Artificial intelligence will help predict certificate failures, detect misconfigurations, and optimize key management.

Post-Quantum Cryptography (PQC) Integration – Organizations will automate the transition to quantum-resistant cryptographic algorithms.

Blockchain-Based Certificate Transparency – Decentralized PKI ecosystems may enhance certificate trust and security verification.

Automating certificate management is essential for modern cybersecurity. By leveraging ACME protocols, cloud-based CMS platforms, and AI-driven automation, organizations can improve certificate security, reduce operational risks, and maintain compliance with evolving industry standards.

Open-Source PKI Solutions

Public Key Infrastructure (PKI) is a foundational security technology that enables secure authentication, encryption, and digital signatures for applications, users, and devices. While many enterprises rely on commercial PKI solutions, open-source PKI platforms provide an alternative that is cost-effective, flexible, and transparent. Open-source PKI solutions allow organizations to deploy and manage certificate authorities (CAs), digital certificates, and cryptographic key management systems without the constraints of proprietary software.

Open-source PKI implementations are widely used in web security, cloud computing, IoT, DevOps environments, and enterprise authentication. Organizations choose open-source PKI for its customizability, community-driven development, and support for open standards. However, deploying and maintaining an open-source PKI solution requires expertise in certificate lifecycle management, cryptographic security, and regulatory compliance.

Advantages of Open-Source PKI Solutions

Many organizations prefer open-source PKI platforms due to their numerous advantages:

Cost Savings – Open-source PKI eliminates licensing fees, reducing operational expenses for small businesses and enterprises.

Transparency and Security – Open-source software allows auditing of source code, ensuring that no hidden vulnerabilities, backdoors, or vendor lock-ins exist.

Flexibility and Customization – Developers can modify and extend open-source PKI solutions to meet specific security policies, compliance requirements, and automation needs.

Community Support and Collaboration – Open-source PKI projects benefit from community-driven development, continuous improvements, and contributions from cybersecurity experts.

Compliance with Open Standards – Many open-source PKI solutions support X.509 certificates, TLS/SSL encryption, OCSP, and ACME protocols, ensuring interoperability with browsers, servers, and cloud providers.

Popular Open-Source PKI Solutions

Several open-source PKI platforms offer comprehensive features for certificate authority (CA) management, certificate issuance, revocation, and key lifecycle management.

1. EJBCA (Enterprise Java Beans Certificate Authority)

EJBCA is one of the most powerful and widely adopted open-source PKI platforms, designed for enterprise, government, and cloud environments.

Key Features:

Supports multi-tier CA hierarchies (Root CA, Intermediate CA).

Provides certificate lifecycle automation for large-scale deployments.

Integrates with Active Directory (AD), HSMs, and OpenID Connect.

Supports multiple cryptographic standards, including RSA, ECC, and post-quantum cryptography (PQC).

Use Cases:

Large enterprises managing internal PKI infrastructure.

Government agencies issuing digital certificates for citizens and e-Government services.

Cloud-based PKI deployments with automated certificate issuance.

2. OpenXPKI

OpenXPKI is a feature-rich open-source PKI solution known for its modular architecture and automation-friendly design.

Key Features:

Uses a REST API for easy integration with DevOps and cloud environments.

Supports ACME (Automated Certificate Management Environment) for automated TLS certificate issuance and renewal.

Provides Role-Based Access Control (RBAC) for secure CA administration.

Use Cases:

Automating PKI for Kubernetes, microservices, and CI/CD pipelines.

Enabling self-service certificate issuance for enterprise IT teams.

3. Dogtag PKI

Dogtag PKI is a Red Hat-sponsored open-source PKI solution designed for Linux-based enterprise environments. It is widely used in identity and access management (IAM) applications.

Key Features:

Provides high-availability CA clustering for scalability.

Supports smart card authentication, digital signatures, and timestamping.

Integrates with FreeIPA for enterprise identity management.

Use Cases:

Government and military organizations requiring high-security PKI infrastructure.

Enterprises implementing PKI for employee authentication and S/MIME email encryption.

4. Step CA (Smallstep)

Step CA is a lightweight, cloud-native PKI designed for DevOps, containers, and automated certificate issuance.

Key Features:

Supports ACME protocol for automated TLS certificate issuance.

Provides mTLS authentication for securing API gateways, Kubernetes clusters, and IoT devices.

Includes command-line tools for developers to generate and manage certificates.

Use Cases:

Securing Kubernetes workloads with mutual TLS authentication.

Automating certificate management in cloud and CI/CD environments.

5. Lemur (Netflix PKI Automation)

Lemur is an open-source certificate management platform developed by Netflix, designed for automating certificate issuance and renewal across enterprise environments.

Key Features:

Automates TLS/SSL certificate provisioning for cloud applications.

Integrates with HashiCorp Vault, AWS ACM, and enterprise CAs.

Provides a dashboard for monitoring and auditing certificate lifecycles.

Use Cases:

Large-scale certificate automation in cloud and hybrid environments.

Security operations teams managing enterprise PKI compliance.

Challenges of Deploying Open-Source PKI

While open-source PKI solutions offer flexibility and cost savings, they also present challenges:

Complex Setup and Configuration – Open-source PKI platforms require expertise in cryptography, CA hierarchies, and certificate policies.

Security and Compliance Management – Organizations must ensure proper key management, certificate revocation, and policy enforcement to remain compliant with ISO 27001, NIST, PCI DSS, and GDPR.

Scaling for Large Deployments – Some open-source PKI solutions may require customization or additional tooling to scale effectively in enterprise and cloud environments.

Limited Enterprise Support – Unlike commercial PKI vendors, open-source PKI projects rely on community support and contributions, which may not provide fast troubleshooting and security patches.

Best Practices for Implementing Open-Source PKI

To ensure a secure and efficient open-source PKI deployment, organizations should follow best practices:

Use a Multi-Tier CA Architecture – Deploy separate Root CAs, Intermediate CAs, and issuing CAs to enhance security and scalability.

Store Private Keys Securely – Use HSMs (Hardware Security Modules) or cloud-based key management services (KMS) to protect cryptographic keys.

Automate Certificate Management – Implement ACME-based automation to reduce human errors and prevent expired certificates.

Monitor and Audit PKI Activity – Use logging and SIEM solutions to track certificate issuance, revocations, and access control.

Regularly Update Cryptographic Policies – Ensure compliance with modern cryptographic standards (RSA-4096, ECC-384, TLS 1.3, SHA-256) and prepare for post-quantum cryptography (PQC).

The Future of Open-Source PKI

As organizations embrace cloud computing, DevOps, and IoT security, open-source PKI solutions will continue to evolve. Emerging trends include:

Integration with Blockchain-Based PKI for decentralized identity management.

Post-Quantum Cryptography (PQC) Support to resist future quantum-based attacks.

AI-Powered Certificate Lifecycle Management for automated threat detection.

Open-source PKI solutions provide a flexible, transparent, and cost-effective approach to securing digital identities and encrypted communications. By implementing best practices and leveraging automated certificate management tools, organizations can deploy a scalable and secure PKI infrastructure tailored to their needs.

Commercial PKI Solutions and Vendors

Public Key Infrastructure (PKI) is essential for securing digital communications, encrypting sensitive data, and authenticating users and devices. While some organizations opt for open-source PKI solutions, many enterprises and government institutions choose commercial PKI solutions due to their scalability, advanced security features, regulatory compliance, and enterprise support. Commercial

PKI vendors provide fully managed platforms that simplify certificate lifecycle management, automation, and integration with enterprise applications.

Advantages of Commercial PKI Solutions

Enterprises and organizations choose commercial PKI vendors for several reasons:

Scalability and High Availability – Commercial PKI platforms support millions of certificates and offer cloud-native, on-premises, and hybrid deployments.

Compliance and Regulatory Support – Many vendors provide built-in compliance tools for HIPAA, PCI DSS, eIDAS, GDPR, FIPS 140-2, and NIST standards.

Automation and Integration – Commercial PKI solutions integrate with Active Directory, DevOps workflows, cloud platforms, and identity management systems.

Advanced Security Features – Enterprise PKI solutions include hardware security module (HSM) integration, post-quantum cryptography (PQC) readiness, and AI-driven certificate monitoring.

Dedicated Enterprise Support – Unlike open-source PKI, commercial solutions offer 24/7 customer support, security patches, and compliance updates.

Leading Commercial PKI Vendors

Several vendors dominate the PKI market, offering certificate management, cloud PKI, automated TLS certificate issuance, and secure authentication solutions.

1. DigiCert

DigiCert is one of the most recognized PKI vendors, offering enterprise-grade TLS/SSL certificates, certificate lifecycle management, and post-quantum cryptography solutions.

Key Features:

DigiCert CertCentral automates certificate issuance, renewal, and revocation.

Secure Site Pro TLS Certificates with post-quantum cryptographic support.

Integration with Microsoft Active Directory Certificate Services (AD CS).

Managed PKI for IoT security and enterprise authentication.

Use Cases:

Enterprises managing large-scale digital certificate deployments.

Securing IoT devices, VPN authentication, and cloud applications.

2. Entrust

Entrust provides a full suite of PKI and identity security solutions, catering to governments, financial institutions, and cloud service providers.

Key Features:

Cloud and On-Premises PKI with full certificate lifecycle automation.

Trusted digital identity management for employees, devices, and mobile applications.

HSM Integration for secure private key storage.

Multi-cloud PKI support, integrating with AWS, Azure, and Google Cloud.

Use Cases:

Government agencies requiring FIPS 140-2 and NIST-compliant PKI.

Financial institutions securing transactions, identity verification, and compliance.

3. GlobalSign

GlobalSign is a trusted Certificate Authority (CA) that provides enterprise PKI, digital signatures, and cloud-based certificate management.

Key Features:

Managed PKI (MPKI) for automated certificate issuance and tracking.

Identity and Access Management (IAM) integration with Zero Trust security models.

IoT PKI solutions for securing smart devices and industrial systems.

ACME protocol support for automating TLS certificate renewals.

Use Cases:

Enterprises needing scalable certificate automation.

Securing e-commerce platforms, enterprise networks, and IoT ecosystems.

4. Venafi

Venafi specializes in machine identity management and automated certificate security, helping organizations prevent outages, mitigate threats, and maintain compliance.

Key Features:

Venafi Trust Protection Platform automates certificate discovery, issuance, and revocation.

TLS Certificate Monitoring with AI-driven anomaly detection.

Cloud-native PKI with multi-cloud integration (AWS, Azure, Kubernetes).

Cryptographic policy enforcement ensuring compliance with NIST, PCI DSS, and GDPR.

Use Cases:

Financial services, telecom, and critical infrastructure providers needing automated PKI governance.

Organizations securing DevOps, cloud applications, and CI/CD pipelines.

5. Microsoft Active Directory Certificate Services (AD CS)

Microsoft AD CS provides enterprise PKI solutions for Windows environments, integrating certificate-based authentication, encryption, and smart card authentication.

Key Features:

Enterprise-wide certificate issuance and management for Windows-based networks.

Group Policy integration to enforce security policies for certificates.

Support for Wi-Fi authentication, VPN security, and device management.

Use Cases:

Organizations using Microsoft Active Directory for authentication and encryption.

Enterprise PKI for Windows Server-based IT infrastructures.

6. AWS Certificate Manager (ACM)

AWS Certificate Manager provides cloud-based PKI and automated TLS/SSL certificate deployment for applications running in Amazon Web Services (AWS).

Key Features:

Automated TLS/SSL certificate provisioning and renewal for AWS services.

Integration with Amazon CloudFront, Elastic Load Balancer (ELB), and API Gateway.

ACME protocol support for automated certificate issuance.

Use Cases:

Enterprises running multi-cloud PKI for AWS-based applications.

Securing serverless functions, API communications, and cloud workloads.

Challenges in Implementing Commercial PKI Solutions

Despite their advantages, commercial PKI solutions present challenges, including:

Cost of Licensing and Subscription Fees – Commercial PKI vendors charge for certificates, managed services, and premium features, making them expensive for startups and small businesses.

Complex Integration with Legacy Systems – Many enterprises use outdated applications that require custom PKI integrations to function securely.

Vendor Lock-in Risks – Relying on a single PKI provider may limit flexibility and increase switching costs in the future.

Scaling Challenges in Multi-Cloud Environments – Enterprises operating hybrid cloud infrastructures may require custom PKI policies to manage certificates across AWS, Azure, Google Cloud, and on-premises systems.

Best Practices for Deploying Commercial PKI Solutions

Organizations can maximize the security and efficiency of commercial PKI solutions by following best practices:

Define a Clear Certificate Policy – Establish rules for certificate issuance, renewal, revocation, and cryptographic key lifetimes.

Automate Certificate Lifecycle Management – Use ACME-based automation and TLS monitoring tools to prevent outages and security gaps.

Implement Role-Based Access Control (RBAC) – Restrict access to certificate authorities (CAs) and private keys to minimize insider threats.

Monitor and Audit PKI Activity – Use SIEM (Security Information and Event Management) solutions to detect anomalies in certificate usage.

Adopt Post-Quantum Cryptography (PQC) Readiness – Prepare for quantum-safe encryption by evaluating lattice-based and hash-based cryptographic algorithms.

The Future of Commercial PKI Solutions

The evolution of cybersecurity threats and compliance mandates will drive new innovations in commercial PKI, including:

AI-Powered Certificate Intelligence – AI-driven PKI platforms will enhance certificate risk detection, anomaly monitoring, and automated threat response.

Decentralized PKI (dPKI) and Blockchain-Based Identity Management – Future PKI solutions may leverage blockchain for tamper-proof digital identities and self-sovereign identity verification.

Post-Quantum Cryptography (PQC) Integration – Vendors will transition to quantum-resistant cryptographic standards to mitigate future quantum threats.

Commercial PKI solutions offer enterprise-grade security, automation, and compliance for organizations requiring scalable, trusted, and fully managed PKI infrastructure. By selecting the right vendor, automating certificate management, and implementing security best practices, businesses can enhance cybersecurity, prevent outages, and future-proof their encryption strategies.

Real-World PKI Case Studies

Public Key Infrastructure (PKI) is a critical technology for securing digital transactions, encrypting sensitive data, and authenticating users and devices. Organizations across various industries rely on PKI to protect financial transactions, government communications, healthcare records, cloud infrastructures, and IoT ecosystems. By examining real-world case studies, we can better understand how PKI is implemented in different sectors, the challenges organizations face, and the benefits of a well-structured PKI deployment.

Case Study 1: PKI in Financial Services – Securing Online Banking Transactions

A multinational bank with operations in multiple countries needed to enhance the security of its online banking and payment systems. The bank was facing increasing threats from phishing attacks, man-in-the-middle (MITM) attacks, and identity fraud. Additionally, regulatory requirements such as PSD2 (Payment Services Directive 2) and PCI DSS (Payment Card Industry Data Security Standard) required strong authentication and encryption for financial transactions.

Challenges:

Implementing strong customer authentication (SCA) for online banking without compromising user experience.

Preventing fraudulent transactions and ensuring data confidentiality.

Managing a large volume of digital certificates for customer authentication, TLS encryption, and code signing.

PKI Implementation:

The bank deployed PKI-based client authentication using digital certificates stored on smart cards and mobile devices.

TLS/SSL certificates were issued and managed using an automated certificate management system to secure banking portals and APIs.

PKI-backed digital signatures were introduced for secure fund transfers and online contracts.

The bank integrated mutual TLS (mTLS) authentication between its internal systems and third-party financial service providers.

Results:

A 98% reduction in phishing-related fraud cases due to PKI-based authentication.

Full compliance with PSD2 and PCI DSS encryption requirements.

Improved customer trust and adoption of digital banking services.

Case Study 2: Government PKI – Implementing National Digital Identity

A European government launched a national digital identity program to enable secure electronic transactions for citizens, businesses, and government agencies. The goal was to provide trusted digital identities for e-Government services, tax filings, healthcare access, and secure communication.

Challenges:

Ensuring high security for digital identity issuance and authentication.

Preventing identity fraud while ensuring ease of use for citizens.

Complying with eIDAS (Electronic Identification, Authentication and Trust Services) regulations for legal recognition of digital signatures.

PKI Implementation:

A centralized Certificate Authority (CA) was established to issue qualified digital certificates for national ID cards.

Citizens were provided with smart cards and mobile-based PKI certificates for secure authentication and digital signing.

Government websites and online services enforced TLS encryption and certificate-based authentication for secure access.

Digital signatures were implemented for electronic contracts, tax declarations, and medical prescriptions.

Results:

Over 20 million citizens enrolled in the national digital identity program.

Increased adoption of secure e-Government services, reducing administrative costs and paperwork.

Enhanced security for online transactions, reducing identity theft and fraud.

Case Study 3: PKI in Healthcare – Securing Electronic Health Records (EHRs)

A major hospital network needed to secure patient data and medical communications while complying with HIPAA (Health Insurance Portability and Accountability Act) regulations. The hospital was experiencing data breaches, unauthorized access to medical records, and phishing attacks targeting doctors and staff.

Challenges:

Preventing unauthorized access to electronic health records (EHRs).

Ensuring secure communication between hospitals, clinics, and laboratories.

Protecting medical devices and IoT-enabled healthcare equipment.

PKI Implementation:

Digital certificates were issued to doctors, nurses, and administrators for secure authentication.

TLS/SSL encryption was deployed for EHR platforms, ensuring that patient data remained confidential during transmission.

S/MIME email encryption was enforced to prevent phishing attacks targeting healthcare professionals.

PKI was integrated with IoT medical devices to authenticate device communications and ensure data integrity.

Results:

A 75% reduction in unauthorized access incidents to patient data.

Improved compliance with HIPAA security standards.

Enhanced security for telemedicine consultations and remote healthcare services.

Case Study 4: Cloud PKI – Securing a Multi-Cloud Infrastructure

A global technology company migrated its infrastructure to multi-cloud environments (AWS, Azure, Google Cloud) but faced security challenges in managing identities, encrypting communications, and securing DevOps workflows.

Challenges:

Managing a large volume of TLS/SSL certificates across multiple cloud providers.

Ensuring secure API authentication and mutual TLS (mTLS) communication between cloud services.

Automating certificate issuance and renewal to prevent expired certificates from disrupting operations.

PKI Implementation:

The company deployed a cloud-based PKI solution integrated with AWS Certificate Manager (ACM) and Azure Key Vault.

ACME protocol was used to automate certificate issuance and renewal for DevOps and microservices deployments.

Mutual TLS (mTLS) authentication was enforced for secure API transactions between cloud applications, Kubernetes clusters, and internal services.

Certificate lifecycle management was automated to track expiration dates and prevent outages.

Results:

Improved multi-cloud security by enforcing certificate-based authentication and encryption.

A 90% reduction in downtime caused by expired certificates.

Strengthened DevOps security by ensuring that cloud workloads were properly authenticated.

Case Study 5: PKI for IoT – Securing Smart Cities

A smart city initiative deployed IoT devices, smart sensors, and automated infrastructure to improve traffic management, public safety, and energy efficiency. However, the city faced growing cybersecurity threats, including device spoofing, data interception, and unauthorized access.

Challenges:

Authenticating thousands of IoT sensors and smart infrastructure devices.

Securing real-time data transmission between IoT devices and central control systems.

Preventing unauthorized access to public transportation, surveillance, and energy management systems.

PKI Implementation:

A PKI-based IoT identity framework was implemented to issue digital certificates for each IoT device.

All device communications were secured using TLS encryption and mutual authentication.

Automated certificate revocation ensured that compromised IoT devices were immediately deactivated.

Edge computing security was enhanced with PKI-backed identity verification for decentralized IoT nodes.

Results:

Secure and tamper-proof IoT communications across the city's infrastructure.

A 50% reduction in cyberattacks targeting smart city devices.

Improved public trust in smart infrastructure security.

These case studies demonstrate the versatility and critical importance of PKI across industries. From financial transactions and healthcare security to cloud infrastructures and smart cities, PKI remains an essential foundation for trust, authentication, and encryption in digital environments.

Troubleshooting PKI Issues

Public Key Infrastructure (PKI) is a fundamental security framework used for encrypting communications, authenticating identities, and securing transactions. However, PKI environments can be complex, and misconfigurations, expired certificates, or key management issues can lead to security vulnerabilities, authentication failures, and service disruptions. Identifying and resolving PKI issues requires a deep understanding of certificate management, trust chains, revocation mechanisms, and cryptographic policies. Troubleshooting PKI problems involves diagnosing issues in certificate authorities (CAs), digital certificates, private key storage, and encryption protocols to restore secure operations efficiently.

One of the most common PKI issues arises from expired or invalid certificates. When a certificate expires, users and services relying on it may experience authentication failures, application errors, or blocked access to encrypted data. Expired certificates often cause disruptions in websites, VPNs, email encryption, and enterprise authentication systems. The best way to prevent such issues is to implement automated certificate lifecycle management, where expiration alerts and auto-renewal mechanisms help avoid downtime. In cases where an expired certificate has already caused an outage, immediate renewal and distribution of the new certificate must be performed while ensuring all dependent systems are updated.

Another frequent problem in PKI implementations is trust chain validation errors. These occur when a system cannot establish a trusted path between an issued certificate and a trusted root CA. The issue may be due to a missing or incorrectly installed intermediate CA certificate, a revoked certificate in the chain, or a mismatch between certificate policies. Verifying the certificate path using tools like OpenSSL,

Microsoft CertUtil, or browser debugging tools can help identify where the trust chain breaks. If an intermediate CA certificate is missing, manually importing it into the system's trusted certificate store can resolve the issue. If a certificate has been revoked or its chain is incomplete, reissuing a new certificate may be required.

Private key mismanagement is another critical PKI challenge. A certificate without its corresponding private key cannot be used for authentication or encryption. This problem often arises when migrating servers, restoring backups, or manually importing certificates. If a private key is lost, it cannot be recovered, and a new certificate must be issued. To prevent private key-related issues, organizations should enforce secure key storage practices using hardware security modules (HSMs) or encrypted key stores. Additionally, ensuring that private keys are securely backed up and properly exported when migrating certificates can help avoid service disruptions.

Certificate revocation issues can lead to unauthorized access or failure in validating digital signatures. PKI systems use Certificate Revocation Lists (CRLs) and the Online Certificate Status Protocol (OCSP) to check whether a certificate is still valid. If a system cannot access CRL or OCSP servers due to network issues, firewalls, or outdated revocation lists, it may reject otherwise valid certificates or allow revoked certificates to be trusted. Diagnosing revocation problems involves checking CRL and OCSP configurations, ensuring that endpoints can connect to revocation servers, and verifying that CRLs are regularly updated. If a revoked certificate is still being accepted, forcing a CRL update or manually disabling the affected certificate may be necessary.

TLS handshake failures are another common issue in PKI environments, especially when configuring secure communication channels between web servers, clients, and APIs. These failures may occur due to mismatched TLS versions, unsupported cipher suites, expired or untrusted certificates, or incorrect key exchange settings. Analyzing server logs, using tools like Wireshark or OpenSSL to inspect TLS traffic, and verifying certificate validity can help diagnose handshake failures. Updating TLS configurations to enforce strong encryption protocols and ensuring that both client and server support the same cryptographic standards can resolve many handshake issues.

Misconfigured certificate policies and extended key usage attributes can also cause authentication failures in enterprise environments. Some applications, such as VPN clients, email encryption systems, or digital signatures, require certificates with specific key usage extensions. If a certificate lacks the necessary attributes or includes incompatible extensions, it may be rejected by the application. Checking the certificate attributes using tools like OpenSSL or Microsoft Management Console (MMC) can help verify whether the certificate meets the required policies. If necessary, a new certificate with the correct key usage settings must be issued by the CA.

Time synchronization discrepancies between systems can lead to PKI-related authentication errors. Certificates have validity periods, and if a server or client system has an incorrect time setting, it may consider a valid certificate as expired or not yet valid. Ensuring that all systems synchronize with a reliable Network Time Protocol (NTP) server prevents such issues. Diagnosing time-related certificate errors involves checking system clocks, manually adjusting time settings if necessary, and verifying that all PKI components operate with synchronized timestamps.

Enterprise environments that integrate PKI with Active Directory often encounter smart card authentication or Kerberos authentication failures due to certificate mapping issues. If a user's certificate is not properly linked to their Active Directory account or if the authentication policies do not match the certificate attributes, authentication will fail. Checking Active Directory logs, verifying certificate mappings, and ensuring that group policies correctly enforce PKI authentication can help resolve these issues.

Automation errors in certificate provisioning and renewal can also cause PKI disruptions. Organizations that use automated certificate management systems may experience issues if scripts fail, certificate requests are misconfigured, or API integrations with CAs break. Diagnosing these issues requires reviewing automation logs, ensuring that API connections are functioning properly, and validating that automated workflows correctly follow issuance policies.

Network connectivity issues can impact PKI services, especially in distributed environments where certificate authorities, OCSP responders, and revocation servers operate across multiple locations. If firewalls or proxies block communication between PKI components, certificate validation may fail. Troubleshooting network-related PKI issues involves checking firewall rules, using network diagnostic tools like traceroute and telnet, and ensuring that necessary PKI services are reachable.

Logging and monitoring play a crucial role in PKI troubleshooting. Organizations should maintain detailed logs of certificate issuance, revocation, authentication attempts, and system errors. Security Information and Event Management (SIEM) tools can aggregate PKI-related logs and help identify anomalies in certificate usage. Regular audits of PKI infrastructure, including compliance checks and penetration testing, ensure that potential issues are detected and resolved before they cause security breaches.

A well-structured PKI troubleshooting approach involves identifying the root cause of the issue, validating certificate configurations, analyzing cryptographic policies, and ensuring network connectivity. By implementing best practices in certificate lifecycle management, automating certificate renewal, and maintaining secure key storage, organizations can minimize PKI-related errors and maintain a reliable, trusted digital security infrastructure.

PKI Performance Optimization

Public Key Infrastructure (PKI) is a critical component of securing communications, transactions, and identities across many industries. However, PKI can be complex, and as its scope grows within an organization, so does the need for performance optimization. Whether it's the efficient handling of large numbers of certificates, the scalability of infrastructure, or the speed of cryptographic operations, performance issues in PKI can impact user experience, cause delays, and increase system costs. Optimizing the performance of PKI systems is essential to maintaining the seamless operation of secure applications, networks, and services.

PKI performance can be compromised by several factors, including certificate issuance time, certificate revocation processing, encryption and decryption delays, and scalability issues when dealing with a large number of devices or users. The process of issuing and verifying certificates, managing cryptographic keys, and performing encryption/decryption operations can be resource-intensive. When handling thousands or millions of certificates across an enterprise, these processes can create significant bottlenecks that affect not only security but also the availability and performance of critical systems. Organizations must address these issues to ensure that PKI does not become a performance hindrance to their security infrastructure.

A common area where performance optimization is needed is the certificate issuance process. The time it takes to generate a certificate, validate the requester's identity, and issue the final digital certificate can vary widely depending on the PKI deployment and the Certificate Authority (CA) infrastructure. Manual certificate issuance can significantly slow down the process, especially in a large organization where certificates need to be issued in large numbers. One way to address this issue is by automating certificate lifecycle management through automated certificate issuance and renewal. By using automation tools such as ACME (Automated Certificate Management Environment) or certificate management platforms that integrate with internal systems and cloud services, organizations can streamline the certificate issuance process. Automation ensures that certificates are issued quickly and accurately without requiring manual intervention, improving the overall efficiency of the PKI deployment.

The revocation process is another area where performance issues may arise. Revoked certificates must be tracked and communicated to the systems that rely on them, so that they are not mistakenly trusted. However, handling Certificate Revocation Lists (CRLs) and Online Certificate Status Protocol (OCSP) queries can introduce delays, especially in large-scale environments where certificates are frequently revoked. CRLs, when not managed properly, can grow large and become cumbersome to download and process. To optimize this process, it is important to periodically update CRLs and limit their size by setting appropriate expiration times for certificates. Another solution is to implement OCSP stapling, a technique that allows servers to include the status of certificates directly in their responses, reducing the need for clients to query external OCSP servers. By enabling OCSP stapling and managing CRLs efficiently, organizations can significantly reduce the latency associated with certificate revocation checks.

The performance of cryptographic operations, particularly encryption and decryption, can also impact PKI performance. Cryptographic algorithms used in PKI, such as RSA, ECC, and DSA, require significant computational resources, especially for large-scale environments. The process of encrypting and decrypting data or authenticating users using these algorithms can introduce delays, particularly when large numbers of users or devices are involved. One strategy to optimize cryptographic performance is to use hardware acceleration, such as Hardware Security Modules (HSMs) or Trusted Platform Modules (TPMs), to offload computationally expensive cryptographic operations. By leveraging hardware-based cryptographic solutions, organizations can achieve faster encryption/decryption speeds, significantly reducing latency and improving overall performance.

In addition to hardware acceleration, choosing the right cryptographic algorithms and key lengths can also optimize performance. While RSA is widely used, it is known for being slower compared to more modern algorithms like Elliptic Curve Cryptography (ECC), which offers the same level of security with much smaller key sizes. Organizations can optimize PKI performance by adopting ECC-based certificates for public key exchanges and digital signatures, reducing the computational load on both servers and clients. In environments where high throughput is required, organizations can also consider using post-quantum cryptography (PQC) algorithms that are designed to be efficient and secure against future quantum attacks, although PQC is still in its early stages of deployment.

Scalability is another critical aspect of PKI performance, particularly in organizations that manage a large number of devices, users, and applications. As the number of certificates grows, managing the PKI infrastructure becomes increasingly complex. Distributed CA systems can help organizations scale their PKI by decentralizing the certificate issuance process, enabling multiple CAs to operate in parallel and handle different parts of the network. This reduces the load on a single CA and allows the PKI system to scale horizontally. Cloud-based PKI solutions can also provide the necessary scalability, with the added benefit of being able to dynamically adjust resources as the number of certificates or users fluctuates. Additionally, implementing a centralized certificate management platform that integrates with existing IT systems can improve scalability by providing a single interface to monitor and manage certificates across the entire infrastructure.

Optimizing PKI performance also involves optimizing the network infrastructure that supports PKI services. Latency in PKI systems can be caused by network delays in certificate requests, verifications, and revocation checks. To address this, organizations should ensure that PKI-related services such as CAs, OCSP responders, and CRL distribution points are located in geographically distributed data centers, ideally in locations close to users or devices. This reduces the time it takes to access PKI services and improves response times for certificate validation. Additionally, leveraging content delivery networks (CDNs) for distributing certificates and revocation lists can help reduce latency, ensuring that users have quick access to up-to-date certificate information.

Lastly, regular monitoring and auditing of PKI performance is essential for identifying bottlenecks and improving efficiency. By using real-time monitoring tools that track certificate usage, expiration, and revocation, organizations can identify potential issues before they affect system performance. Additionally, conducting performance audits and simulating high-volume certificate issuance scenarios can help organizations understand the scalability limits of their PKI infrastructure and plan for future growth.

PKI performance optimization is crucial for maintaining secure, efficient, and scalable digital security solutions. By addressing key areas such as certificate issuance and revocation, cryptographic operations, scalability, and network infrastructure, organizations can significantly improve the performance of their PKI systems while ensuring they meet security, compliance, and operational requirements. Regular performance monitoring, automation, and hardware acceleration will enable enterprises to handle the increasing demand for certificates and maintain optimal security at all times.

Future Trends in PKI Technology

Public Key Infrastructure (PKI) has been an essential part of digital security for decades. It is the backbone of many cryptographic operations, ensuring the authenticity of identities, securing communications, and enabling encrypted data transfers. As the digital landscape evolves, PKI faces new challenges and opportunities. The increasing demand for cloud-based services, IoT devices, and advanced cryptography are driving innovations in PKI technology. Future trends in PKI will focus on scalability, automation, the integration of post-quantum cryptography (PQC), and the adaptation to blockchain and decentralized models. These developments will enhance security, streamline management processes, and address new vulnerabilities introduced by technological advancements.

One of the most pressing challenges PKI faces is scalability. As enterprises move more of their services to the cloud, manage a growing number of IoT devices, and expand their digital infrastructure, traditional PKI systems are struggling to keep pace with the sheer volume of certificates that need to be issued, renewed, and revoked. Organizations now require PKI solutions that can easily handle millions of certificates across cloud environments, multiple data centers, and an ever-growing number of devices. Future PKI technologies will prioritize automation to streamline certificate management, ensuring that the process of issuing, renewing, and revoking certificates can occur without manual intervention. Automation will be vital for reducing the complexity of certificate management while improving the speed and accuracy of issuing and validating certificates in increasingly dynamic digital environments.

Another significant trend is the move towards quantum-resilient encryption. Quantum computing promises to revolutionize computing power, but it also introduces potential risks to traditional encryption algorithms used in PKI, such as RSA and Elliptic Curve Cryptography (ECC). Quantum computers could theoretically break the public key cryptographic algorithms that underpin PKI systems, rendering current encryption methods obsolete. As a result, post-quantum cryptography (PQC) is emerging as a key focus area. PQC involves developing cryptographic algorithms that are resistant to attacks by quantum computers. The integration of PQC into PKI will be crucial in securing future communications and ensuring long-term data protection. This transition to quantum-safe PKI will involve adopting algorithms based on lattice-based cryptography, hash-based signatures, and code-based cryptography, which are believed to be secure against quantum attacks. The industry is actively researching these algorithms, and standards are expected to be finalized within the next few years, enabling the transition to a quantum-resistant PKI ecosystem.

The rise of blockchain and decentralized technologies is also influencing the future of PKI. Blockchain offers immutable, tamper-proof records of transactions, which has led to the exploration of its integration with PKI for decentralized identity management. Traditional PKI relies on centralized Certificate Authorities (CAs) to issue and validate certificates. However, blockchain technology allows for decentralized PKI, where trust is distributed across a network of nodes rather than relying on a single CA. This shift could address concerns about the potential vulnerabilities of centralized authorities and provide a more resilient and transparent system for issuing and verifying certificates. Blockchain-based PKI solutions could significantly improve the security and privacy of digital identities and transactions, making it harder for malicious actors to compromise the system.

Moreover, as digital transformation accelerates, the need for strong authentication systems will continue to rise. PKI will increasingly play a central role in enabling multi-factor authentication (MFA) and identity federation. The use of smart cards, biometric data, and digital certificates for secure authentication is becoming more common in high-security environments. Future PKI systems will be designed to support these advanced authentication methods, ensuring seamless single sign-on (SSO) experiences across a wide range of platforms, including cloud applications, mobile devices, and IoT ecosystems. As users and organizations embrace more digital services, secure and efficient user authentication will be vital in preventing unauthorized access to sensitive systems.

The growing complexity of managing IoT devices will also be a significant driver of change in PKI technology. With billions of devices being connected to the internet, many of which are low-powered and resource-constrained, securing these devices using traditional PKI methods can be inefficient and cumbersome. In the future, PKI solutions will need to adapt to the unique challenges posed by IoT, including lightweight cryptographic protocols, efficient key management, and the need for end-to-end security between devices and the cloud. PKI will play a crucial role in authenticating devices, securing communication between them, and ensuring that only trusted devices are allowed to interact within a network.

Furthermore, cloud-native PKI solutions will become more prevalent as organizations continue to move to the cloud. Cloud-based PKI services provide the flexibility, scalability, and cost-effectiveness needed to manage certificates in dynamic, distributed environments. These solutions allow businesses to issue, manage, and renew certificates across multiple cloud platforms, reducing the overhead of maintaining an on-premises PKI infrastructure. Future cloud-native PKI solutions will integrate seamlessly with DevOps pipelines, microservices architectures, and serverless computing, enabling automatic certificate rotation and management for distributed systems.

AI and machine learning technologies are also beginning to play a role in PKI performance and management. These technologies can be used to enhance threat detection, anomaly monitoring, and predictive maintenance within PKI systems. By analyzing patterns in certificate usage, AI systems could detect suspicious activities, such as unusual certificate requests or unauthorized certificate issuance, and trigger automatic responses to prevent potential breaches. Over time, AI and machine learning will likely be integrated into PKI solutions to increase efficiency, automation, and security monitoring.

Finally, the user experience with PKI systems is expected to improve. As organizations implement PKI in more user-facing applications, there will be a stronger focus on making certificate management and authentication processes seamless and user-friendly. Future PKI solutions will prioritize usability, reducing the friction typically associated with certificate deployment and authentication, particularly for end-users. For example, advancements in browser-based certificate management and zero-touch certificate provisioning will help users and IT administrators alike deploy and manage certificates with minimal manual effort.

As digital security becomes an increasingly critical concern in the modern world, the evolution of PKI will continue to address new challenges brought on by innovations in technology. From the shift to quantum-resistant cryptography to the rise of decentralized PKI and the integration of AI-powered monitoring, these advancements will ensure that PKI remains a cornerstone of trust and security in the digital era. PKI will play an even more significant role in enabling secure communications, digital transactions, and identity management in a future where cybersecurity threats evolve continuously.

Implementing Zero Trust with PKI

The concept of Zero Trust has emerged as a critical security framework in response to the increasingly sophisticated cyber threats and the evolving nature of enterprise IT infrastructures. Unlike traditional perimeter-based security models, which assume that internal networks are trusted, the Zero Trust model operates on the principle that no entity, whether inside or outside the network, should be trusted by default. Every user, device, application, and network request must be continuously verified before being granted access to resources. Implementing Zero Trust with Public Key Infrastructure (PKI) is an effective way to enforce strict access controls, verify identities, and ensure that every action within a system is authenticated and authorized.

PKI plays a fundamental role in Zero Trust security by ensuring strong authentication and encrypted communication between users, devices, and applications. As organizations transition to cloud services, hybrid environments, and remote workforces, PKI enables the implementation of robust identity management, secure access, and encryption protocols needed for Zero Trust architectures.

At the heart of Zero Trust is the need for strong, identity-based authentication. Traditional security models often rely on the assumption that once a user is authenticated, they are trusted within the network. Zero Trust, however, requires continuous verification of users, devices, and applications for every access attempt. PKI supports this continuous authentication by utilizing certificates to uniquely identify users and devices. Digital certificates, issued by a trusted Certificate Authority (CA), contain cryptographic keys that are used for authenticating entities within the network. Each certificate is tied to a specific identity, ensuring that access is only granted to legitimate users or devices.

In a Zero Trust model, multi-factor authentication (MFA) is a core requirement. PKI-enabled MFA enhances security by integrating digital certificates with other authentication factors such as biometrics or one-time passcodes (OTPs). A common example is smart card authentication, where users must insert a smart card and enter a PIN to authenticate. The private key stored on the smart card is used in conjunction with the public key of the issuing CA to authenticate the user. This two-factor authentication process ensures that even if a user's password is compromised, unauthorized access is prevented.

As part of a Zero Trust implementation, organizations must enforce the principle of least privilege, meaning that users and devices are only given access to the resources necessary for their roles. **PKI helps achieve this by supporting role-based access control (RBAC). Each certificate can be associated with specific permissions based on the user's role or the device's function. By binding access policies to digital certificates, organizations can ensure that users or devices are restricted from accessing resources beyond what is necessary for their work. This creates a dynamic access model that adapts to the evolving needs of the enterprise while minimizing security risks.

A Zero Trust model also emphasizes the need for encrypted communications across all interactions, both internal and external. Traditional network security models often focus on securing the perimeter, assuming that once users are inside the network, their communications are trusted. However, Zero Trust requires that every interaction be encrypted, even within the internal network. PKI supports this requirement by providing TLS/SSL certificates for encrypting data in transit between users, applications, and servers. By leveraging PKI-based encryption, sensitive information is protected from eavesdropping, regardless of whether the communication is occurring within a trusted internal network or across an untrusted external network.

One of the challenges of implementing Zero Trust with PKI is managing the dynamic and scalable nature of modern enterprise networks, especially in cloud environments or when dealing with remote workers and mobile devices. As employees work from different locations, accessing resources from various devices and applications, traditional network security tools may struggle to keep pace. **PKI's integration with cloud-based services, such as AWS, Azure, and Google Cloud, facilitates secure, identity-based authentication for cloud applications. By using cloud-native PKI solutions, organizations can implement digital certificates for identity verification and establish secure, encrypted channels for remote access to applications. Moreover, PKI systems can be integrated with Identity and Access Management (IAM) solutions to automate certificate provisioning and revocation based on user roles or security policies.

Another key aspect of Zero Trust is the ability to monitor and continuously verify the health of devices and networks. PKI enables this by facilitating secure communications between devices and monitoring systems. For example, IoT devices can be securely authenticated using PKI-based certificates to ensure that only trusted devices can communicate within the network. With PKI-enabled IoT security, devices can be continuously authenticated and monitored, and any compromise or deviation from normal behavior can trigger automatic revocation of certificates or access restrictions. This level of monitoring and automation is essential in a Zero Trust environment, where the security of every device, regardless of location, must be actively managed and continuously assessed.

The concept of micro-segmentation is also critical in Zero Trust, as it involves dividing the network into smaller, isolated segments to limit the spread of attacks. PKI can support micro-segmentation by ensuring that only trusted devices and users are allowed to access specific network segments. Through the use of PKI certificates, network traffic between different segments can be encrypted and authenticated. This prevents unauthorized users or compromised devices from accessing sensitive segments of the network, even if they have successfully infiltrated other areas of the system. By combining PKI with micro-segmentation policies, organizations can ensure that each segment of the network remains secure and isolated, reducing the impact of potential breaches.

As organizations adopt Zero Trust principles, it is important to ensure the effective management of digital certificates within the PKI framework. Certificate lifecycle management—including the issuance, renewal, and revocation of certificates—must be automated to prevent lapses in security. Automated PKI management solutions ensure that certificates are continuously valid, updated as needed, and revoked immediately when no longer required. This is especially important in a Zero Trust environment, where any unauthorized certificate could compromise the entire security posture.

Implementing Zero Trust with PKI requires a comprehensive, multi-layered approach to security, where every identity, device, and communication is authenticated and verified before access is granted. By integrating strong authentication mechanisms, encrypted communications, role-based access control, and continuous monitoring, organizations can build a secure infrastructure that minimizes risks and improves overall security resilience. PKI serves as the backbone for this architecture, providing the identity management, encryption, and trust mechanisms required for a Zero Trust model to function effectively.

PKI Training and Certification Paths

Public Key Infrastructure (PKI) is a critical technology that ensures secure communication, authentication, and encryption in modern networks. As organizations increasingly rely on PKI for securing their digital assets, the demand for skilled professionals who can implement, manage, and maintain PKI systems continues to grow. Training and certification in PKI are essential for individuals seeking to specialize in cryptography, identity management, and digital certificate management. The training paths available for PKI professionals range from foundational concepts to advanced techniques, and obtaining relevant certifications helps validate expertise in the field, ensuring that professionals can contribute effectively to the security needs of their organizations.

The journey to becoming proficient in PKI begins with understanding the core concepts of cryptography, digital certificates, certificate authorities (CAs), and key management. PKI training usually starts with an introduction to cryptography, which is the foundation of PKI systems. This includes an understanding of symmetric and asymmetric encryption, hash functions, digital signatures, and the mathematical principles that support secure communications. A deep understanding of how encryption works and how certificates are used to establish trust is crucial for anyone entering the PKI field. Training in PKI concepts can be found in various online courses, books, and through vendor-specific training programs that focus on the implementation and management of PKI systems in real-world environments.

For those beginning their journey into PKI, there are several foundational training paths that cover both theoretical and practical knowledge. These introductory courses provide a solid understanding of the basic elements of PKI, such as the roles of public and private keys, the significance of Certificate Authorities (CAs), and the purpose of digital certificates. These courses are designed to equip students with the knowledge needed to understand how PKI works in securing web traffic, email communications, virtual private networks (VPNs), and other digital interactions. Many organizations offer such foundational training courses, and these are often the first step for individuals aiming to enter the field of IT security.

Once individuals have a grasp of the basics, they can pursue more advanced training that covers specialized topics within PKI, including certificate lifecycle management, private key protection, revocation mechanisms, and compliance with security standards such as PCI DSS, HIPAA, and eIDAS. Advanced PKI training often focuses on the complexities of managing a large-scale PKI infrastructure and troubleshooting issues that arise in certificate issuance, revocation, and renewal processes. This stage of training often involves hands-on experience with PKI software solutions, including popular platforms such as Microsoft Certificate Services, OpenSSL, EJBCA, and Venafi. Training at this level often includes lab exercises, case studies, and scenarios that simulate real-world challenges encountered when managing certificates and securing digital assets.

For professionals looking to demonstrate their expertise and advance their careers, obtaining certification in PKI is an excellent way to validate skills and knowledge. Several organizations offer PKI-related certifications that are recognized globally and are highly regarded within the industry. The most recognized certifications are typically offered by professional bodies such as (ISC)², CompTIA, and ISACA, as well as by specific PKI software vendors. These certifications not only validate the holder's knowledge and abilities but also show employers that the individual has a proven understanding of key PKI concepts and can contribute to maintaining a secure IT environment.

One well-known certification for individuals pursuing a career in PKI is the Certified Information Systems Security Professional (CISSP) certification. Offered by (ISC)², the CISSP certification covers a wide range of security topics, including PKI. While the CISSP is a broad certification for security professionals, its coverage of cryptography, key management, and certificate-based authentication makes it a strong option for those focused on PKI in a larger security context. The Certified Information Security Manager (CISM) certification, offered by ISACA, also includes components related to PKI, especially in the context of enterprise security and managing the lifecycle of cryptographic keys and certificates.

Another specialized certification is the CompTIA Security+, which is an entry-level certification for IT professionals and covers basic concepts of network security, cryptography, and PKI. This certification provides a solid foundation for those looking to gain practical experience and a deeper understanding of how PKI systems are deployed and maintained within modern IT environments.

For those seeking to specialize specifically in PKI management, certifications offered by PKI vendors are an excellent option. DigiCert, Venafi, and GlobalSign are examples of PKI vendors that provide certification programs designed to teach professionals how to implement and manage their PKI solutions. These vendor-specific certifications are ideal for individuals who want to work directly with particular PKI platforms and are valuable for those aiming to become experts in a specific product or solution.

Another essential certification is the Certified PKI Professional (CPKI), which is offered by several organizations and focuses entirely on PKI technologies. The CPKI certification is designed for professionals who are responsible for deploying, managing, and maintaining PKI systems, and it demonstrates an individual's ability to handle the complexities of running a large-scale PKI infrastructure. This certification covers topics such as digital certificate life cycle management, certificate authority setup, key management, revocation processes, and more.

In addition to technical certifications, there are also certifications focused on security governance and compliance, which are critical in PKI deployments. The Certified in Risk and Information Systems Control (CRISC) certification from ISACA is one such example. While not directly focused on PKI, CRISC demonstrates a professional's ability to manage IT risk and security controls, including the proper implementation and auditing of PKI systems to ensure compliance with relevant regulatory standards.

For individuals who wish to keep pace with the rapid developments in PKI and cryptography, ongoing education is crucial. This includes attending webinars, conferences, and workshops focused on the latest trends and technologies in PKI, cryptographic standards, and regulatory compliance. Keeping up with evolving standards like FIPS 140-3 or emerging technologies such as quantum-resistant cryptography is essential for PKI professionals.

Overall, PKI training and certification paths are designed to help professionals build a strong foundation in PKI concepts and advance to more specialized knowledge of PKI deployment, management, and troubleshooting. By combining theoretical learning with hands-on practice and obtaining recognized certifications, individuals can position themselves as highly qualified experts in the field of digital security.

Conclusion and Final Thoughts on PKI

Public Key Infrastructure (PKI) remains a cornerstone of modern digital security, providing a robust framework for ensuring the confidentiality, integrity, and authenticity of communications and data. As organizations increasingly embrace digital transformation, the demand for secure methods of identity verification, data encryption, and access control continues to rise. PKI, with its foundation in cryptographic principles, plays a central role in addressing these needs by securing everything from email communications and websites to cloud applications and IoT devices. Despite the many advantages PKI offers, it also presents challenges that must be carefully managed. From certificate lifecycle management to scaling in large environments, the need for effective PKI systems has never been greater.

The key benefit of PKI lies in its ability to provide strong encryption and authentication for users, applications, and devices. The technology underpins secure protocols like SSL/TLS, email encryption, and VPN authentication, making it indispensable for securing data as it travels across untrusted networks. With digital certificates, PKI ensures that both the sender and recipient of a message are who they claim to be, and that the data remains protected from tampering during transmission. As cyber threats evolve and become more sophisticated, relying on traditional security mechanisms is no longer sufficient. PKI offers a proactive approach to security that not only secures data in transit but also authenticates devices and identities, reducing the potential for unauthorized access.

As the digital landscape expands, PKI's role extends beyond the traditional IT infrastructure to newer areas like cloud computing, IoT, and mobile devices. Cloud-based services, in particular, demand a level of security that traditional on-premises solutions cannot always provide. PKI enables the seamless integration of encryption and identity management tools within the cloud, making it easier for organizations to protect sensitive information while maintaining flexibility and scalability. In IoT environments, PKI helps secure the vast number of interconnected devices, ensuring that each device is properly authenticated and that communications between devices are encrypted. This level of security is essential as more devices and services become interconnected, creating a more complex and potentially vulnerable digital ecosystem.

The scalability of PKI continues to be an area of development, especially as enterprises increase their adoption of cloud-based technologies and as the number of devices requiring certificates rises. Managing millions of certificates, tracking expiration dates, and ensuring that proper access controls are in place can become overwhelming without the right systems and automation in place. Automation of certificate lifecycle management has become essential to address this challenge. With tools that allow for automated issuance, renewal, and revocation of certificates, organizations can reduce the administrative burden and eliminate the risk of expired certificates causing system failures or security breaches. As the digital world continues to grow, PKI solutions will need to adapt to handle this increasing demand for both security and efficiency.

Despite its strengths, PKI also faces challenges in user adoption and system management. The complexity of implementing and maintaining PKI can be a barrier, especially for smaller organizations or those with limited IT resources. Ensuring proper integration with existing systems and workflows can be a time-consuming task that requires a deep understanding of cryptographic principles and security protocols. Additionally, the need for secure key management— ensuring that private keys are stored securely and not exposed to unauthorized users—remains a critical concern. Implementing Hardware Security Modules (HSMs) and key management systems (KMSs) will be essential for ensuring the integrity of cryptographic keys in the future.

One of the most important challenges facing PKI today is the emergence of quantum computing. Quantum computers have the potential to break current asymmetric cryptographic algorithms like RSA and ECC, rendering the foundations of traditional PKI insecure. This creates a pressing need for post-quantum cryptography (PQC), which seeks to develop encryption methods that are resistant to the power of quantum computation. While quantum computers that can break modern encryption are not yet a reality, the development of quantum-resistant PKI will be critical for the long-term security of digital systems. Transitioning to PQC solutions will require significant research, adaptation, and investment in new technologies. As a result, PKI will need to evolve in response to these emerging threats, ensuring that it remains effective in safeguarding digital assets.

In parallel with quantum computing concerns, the decentralization of identity management through blockchain and distributed ledger technologies represents another trend influencing the future of PKI.

Blockchain technology offers the possibility of decentralized PKI, where trust is distributed rather than relying on a central Certificate Authority (CA). This new approach could offer improved resilience against attacks on individual CAs and enhance transparency in certificate issuance and management. While still in the early stages, the integration of blockchain with PKI may change how digital identity is verified and how certificates are managed in the future.

As cybersecurity threats become more advanced and widespread, organizations will increasingly rely on PKI to secure their networks and digital services. The evolving digital landscape demands that PKI solutions continue to innovate and adapt to new technologies and practices. The future of PKI will likely be shaped by innovations in cryptography, key management, and identity and access management. Automation will play a key role in ensuring that PKI remains manageable and effective as organizations scale, while post-quantum and blockchain technologies may provide additional layers of security to address emerging threats.

The integration of artificial intelligence (AI) and machine learning (ML) into PKI systems is another area of future development. AI and ML have the potential to improve PKI by automating tasks like certificate monitoring, threat detection, and anomaly detection. These technologies can help identify potential vulnerabilities in the PKI system and ensure that organizations remain proactive in responding to emerging security risks. As AI and ML continue to evolve, their integration into PKI could provide significant improvements in risk management, threat detection, and system optimization.

PKI will continue to be a fundamental pillar of cybersecurity in the future, evolving alongside technological advancements and emerging threats. As digital systems grow more complex and interconnected, PKI's role in ensuring security, identity protection, and trusted communications will only increase. The development of new technologies, from quantum-resistant algorithms to decentralized identity management, will drive the next wave of PKI innovation.

www.ingramcontent.com/pod-product-compliance
Lightning Source LLC
LaVergne TN
LVHW022313060326
832902LV00020B/3443